Passionistas Talk!
The Best of
The Passion Point
Interviews
(Volume 2)

By Caren Glasser
and Friends

Published by:
PYP Publishing Group
Address: 11 Valley Club Circle
City, State Zip: Napa, CA 94558
For Further information please visit www.PYPPublishingGroup.com or call: 415-599-4475

Passionistas Talk - The Best of *The Passion Point* Interviews (Volume 2)
©2015 Caren Glasser
All rights reserved.

Cover Design and Editor: Jaqueline Kyle
PYP Publishing Group
www.PYPPublishingGroup.com
First Printing: 2015
ISBN: 0991041658

TABLE OF CONTENTS

Welcome Reader!

This book, *Passionista's Talk!* has been the culmination of an incredible journey for me. I started a series of nationwide speaking events called Promote Your Passion to create a nurturing environment for entrepreneurs. These events helped thousands to find their passion and purpose and created a community of self-proclaimed "passionistas."

The feedback was incredible but many people were not able to travel to our events. To spread the message and continue to inspire our existing passionistas, I created a show called *The Passion Point*. It is a weekly talk show with each week featuring a different talented passionista discussing their journey to self-fulfillment. Each guest is passionate about what they do and is successful in pursuing a career in their field of choice.

What follows is eight NEW incredible entrepreneurs and four hours of interviews transcribed into book format. My hope for you is that you are inspired by the people in these interviews. Some have faced enormous challenges and have thrived in spite of or because of those challenges. Some have taken a chance on themselves with no one else to say, "You can do it." All have had doubts and fears and pressed on even though it would have been easier to quit.

I hope that you are as inspired by them as I am.

This book is meant for you to enjoy their messages at your own pace and take their lessons to heart. Each of us learns in a different way, and for some, the written word is best. May their inspiration light a passion within you.

Your Chief Passionista,

Caren Glasser

SOHAIL KHAN
OCTOBER 29, 2014

Caren: Hello everyone. Caren Glasser here, and welcome to this episode of *The Passion Point*. This is the show where we follow entrepreneurs and Passionistas all around the world who are following their passion and making a living doing what they love.

I am so, so excited to have our guest on today, Sohail Kahn. He's the founder of The Joint Venture Group. We'll talk a little bit about what that means during our discussion.

But a little history about Sohail. Prior to starting The Joint Venture Group, he had had over 15 years of sales, joint venture marketing, and business experience. In 2009, Sohail set himself a challenge to make $1M within 12 months using nothing but his joint venture marketing expertise at building a business without a product.

So without a product, business, or capital, Sohail closed his biggest joint venture to date and went from $0 to $4M in just 30 days. It's now called The Joint Venture Blueprint.

In 2011, Sohail launched MyBrokeringBusiness.com to train individuals worldwide to operate their own six to seven figure joint venture brokerage. There's that word again, *joint venture*. We'll talk about it.

In 2013, Sohail completed his first published book with the late Jay Conrad Levinson, and it was titled *Guerilla Marketing and Joint Ventures* a few weeks before Jay's death. The book is now out, and you're going to have an opportunity to get a copy of this book free as we get there.

I am excited now to welcome Sohail into the show. How are you today Sohail?

Sohail: I'm good Caren. Thank you for having me on the show.

Caren: Well I am truly excited. You and I met several years ago and when I saw that you were doing this, I really wanted to introduce you to our viewers. So we're going to start out as we always do, to get a definition of passion.

Webster's Dictionary says that passion is *an intense driving or overmastering feeling or conviction.* What does passion mean to you?

Sohail: I think passion is the driving force behind what I do, and I do a lot of it because of passion. It's very interesting you talk about passion. I've been on panels for example. I also speak around the world. And there's always been a debate about doing something that you're passionate about. Does it actually pay?

It's an ongoing discussion. If you do something that's passionate, will it pay bills? I don't do that because it pays the bills. But for me I think it's also not only just being passionate about what you do but honing down on that expert skill that you have that can lead into creating a business around which you not only get paid but also that you really love.

4

Caren: I so agree with that. So let's just talk about your journey. How you went from the start of your business life to where you are now. And then we're going to define the word *joint venture*.

So tell us a little bit how you stumbled upon your passion and did it start really, really early as a young child? Or did it start in your teenage years? Or when did it start?

Sohail: Well basically I've always been an entrepreneur since a young age. One of the things I did when I was very young is I used to go to our sweet shop across the road from our house, buy sweets, and sell them for twice what I bought them for at school.

So I've been always involved in doing something in business as an entrepreneur and I've always enjoyed it. I originally trained as an accountant. One of the things from our cultural background where we come from is our parents are always pushing you to be very academic. For example, the list of things that you can do is to either become a doctor, a lawyer, an accountant, or an astronaut.

I didn't really like heights, so I crossed off the astronaut one. I worked for the next 15 years towards becoming an accountant. I qualified as an accountant, but I didn't really enjoy it. My passion wasn't there.

I spent some time working at a very good accountancy firm. I spent a lot of time helping people learn how to use things like the internet, and building relationships, being someone who loved to be around people, a people person.

So I left that job and I did a Master's in International Business and IT. Then straight off that I wrote a thesis on the impact of the internet on the manufacturing industry. I posted that online and I started getting phone calls from dot-com companies, VCs asking me what this new thing called the internet was. This was back in '96, '97.

At that time, I was straight out of doing my Master's, consulting with some very, very big companies. One of my first jobs was with a company called QVC and it was amazing. I had such an amazing time during the latter part of coming up to 2000 where we working with a lot of big companies doing some consulting and marketing and things that I really enjoyed doing.

I'm a very creative person, even though I come from an analytical background. And I have more of a creative spark. So it was very, very enjoyable watching some of the things that we were doing in these companies and the results we were getting.

But in 2000, we had the dot-com bubble burst, and for that reason lost a lot of our clients. We also had Y2K, which was a double whammy. So not only was our business out there in terms of what we do, we were seen as the main cause of Y2K, being computer consultants.

So early 2000, I came across a book written by one of my own mentors, a man called Jay Abraham, who is a marketing genius. And that book was called *How to Get Everything You Can Out of All You've Got*. In that book, Jay spoke about strategic alliances and joint ventures. This really piqued my interest.

That's how I got started in joint ventures. The first joint venture I did was with a company that I approached and we basically had some computer training courses that we were selling online. The company endorsed the product for us to their 150K database and it was phenomenal.

The first year of our little baby business, we did $20-$30K. The second year with our joint venture partnership, we did over $400K. And that for me was how I got hooked on joint venture partnering.

Caren: Wow! - is all I can say.

So what is the definition of joint venture? How would you describe that to somebody if somebody were to say, *okay, you do this. But what is it? What are you exactly doing?*

6

Sohail: That's a good question. When I'm normally speaking on stage or doing a keynote I give the explanation that a joint venture is a collaboration where two or more entities who share a complementary service or database.

So a classic examples is take a bathroom tile manufacturer, and let's take a bathroom suite manufacturer. They both have the same customers they share. But the problem is they see each other as competitors. So sometimes it's hard for two companies to get together.

Instead of seeing your competitors as competition, you should see them as co-opetition. And this is something that Jay used to always promote called "fusion marketing," which is also called joint venture marketing. Someone like me would be a third component in a joint venture. We'd be like the joint venture broker who comes between these two companies, as an unbiased middleman, and helps these two companies come together and cross-promote each other's products to their customer's databases.

Caren: So you're actually showing why it's beneficial to join forces rather than considering that competition is not a good thing. Competition actually can be a phenomenal thing if you have a similar kind of product, as you said.

For example, I'm a book publisher. But we don't edit. So we have a joint venture with someone who is an amazing editor. We send her our clients to do the editing. And then when she's got clients that she's done editing, she sends them to us for publishing.

So would that be a joint venture?

Sohail: That is entirely how a joint venture works. Basically some of the things that you don't have in-house, you can form a partnership and an alliance with another company who can provide that to your customers. At the end of the day your customers are not going elsewhere for that product or service. Basically the cash flow is not going somewhere else.

Caren: So it's not really an affiliate thing. In fact, maybe it's not an affiliate thing.

Sohail: Here's the difference between joint venture partners and affiliates. I get asked this question all the time. When you do a joint venture, you have a long-term commitment with a joint venture partner to work with them on a one-to-one basis.

Affiliates are people who are always looking for the next thing to promote. You won't really have that close relationship with affiliates. While they're promoting your product, they're probably promoting 50 other products at the same time.

That's the difference between working with a joint venture partner and working with an affiliate.

Caren: And that is really a distinct difference between the two things. Quite frankly, I would much prefer to be partnering or joint venturing with somebody rather than get an affiliate link and promote this product or that product, because it becomes, at least to me, kind of disingenuous.

It doesn't feel good. It feels like I am looking for the next best thing because I have nothing of my own that I can promote. So I totally love joint ventures.

Now, you started in 2013 to get this book published with Jay Conrad Levinson. So I have to know - I followed him since the very beginning and he passed away very recently. What was it like to work with Jay Conrad Levinson?

Sohail: Before going through what it was like working with Jay, I'll give you just a brief background to how the book came about and how we actually connected.

So going further on to my story about the first joint venture that I did, I eventually built that computer training website into a company valued at $10M. And in 2006, sold the majority stake to a 160M IT group. Now in 2008 that company went bust, and I lost everything. So I went from being a multi-millionaire to totally broke in 2008.

Then I set myself a challenge in 2009 to make $1M in 12 months and brokered a $1.5M deal. We'll talk more about that later. And that led me to be invited to speak at a lot of events, especially in the US. This is where Jay and I met. Being invited to speak at a lot of events about how I did this phenomenal joint venture deal and how joint ventures work.

So the book I actually wrote about three years ago, but I was looking for someone to collaborate with and partner with, because I practice what I preach, right? I'm a joint venture expert.

I met Jay on a Master Mind cruise. I'm part of a big Master Mind in the US, a $25K Master Mind. And they do a cruise every year for the Master Mind members. One particular year we had two keynote speakers - Michael Gerber of the *E-Myth* and Jay Conrad Levinson of *Guerilla Marketing*.

Now Michael Gerber was very hard to get a hold of, very hard to approach because he had a lot of his entourage. He would come on, do his keynote, and then come off and disappear. Whereas Jay would connect with people and tour the boat and tell us all these amazing stories.

So I was both fortunate enough to connect with Jay on the cruise and spend some time with him and also send him a copy of my book. He loved the book and he said to me, we have to collaborate on things together and do a Guerilla Marketing book.

We signed an agreement almost two years ago. Last year, we completed the book, got it all finished a few weeks before he passed away. So I'm very fortunate and blessed to have had that experience of working with him. And this being the last ever *Guerilla Marketing* book written by Jay or featuring Jay is also a blessing that we can continue his legacy through this book.

Caren: Absolutely. So in fact, you did a joint venture with Jay Conrad Levinson -

Sohail: Correct.

Caren: - which in order to have that Guerilla Marketing brand, which is world-known, but he in turn was able to also present to his readers and customers, who are of course all over the place, the whole concept of joint venturing as well.

Sohail: Correct.

Caren: So kudos to you. That's awesome! And I know that as we get to the end of our interview we're going to give people a link to go and actually get your book for free.

What would you tell people that have stumbled, and they're trying to figure out - you mentioned this earlier - what their passion is and can I even really make a living doing that. What do you tell people?

Sohail: I think one thing you should do on a consistent basis is always test your idea. I got invited to speak in a very large organization recently. They are a very big corporate company with over 7.2M customers. And the biggest question I was getting in the room was from people who wanted to set up their own business. And they had a passion for things like photography, or one guy had a passion for cars.

They wanted to find out how they could test their passion. And it's very easy to do, especially now with social media and using things like Guerrilla Marketing and direct response. Put your ideas out there. One thing you need to be doing obviously, is a survey.

One of the things we do when we launch new business is we do surveys to groups. So go on to Facebook for example, and go to SurveyMonkey. com, grab a free survey, and survey people to see if they would really be interested in your passion and idea. Would they pay for it?

Then in turn offer them something for free, like a free download or a PDF and collect their email addresses. Once you have a substantial number of addresses, then launch your passion, and you'll have instant buyers straightaway.

Caren: Very, very smart. So I'm all about the quotes. I love quotes. Every morning I go and look for a quote that's going to start my day. And today I'd like to share this quote, and then I'm going to ask you to share a quote that really speaks to you.

This one is by Maya Angelou. She writes, *my mission in life is not merely to survive, but to thrive, and to do so with some passion, some compassion, some humor, and some style.*

I love that. It's awesome. What's a favorite quote of yours?

Sohail: My favorite quote is the quote that I live by. And that is give first, ask later. That is something I always do.

You have to come from a position of serving. And you have to try to serve as many people as possible.

One of the things I always say to people is: what are you doing for other people? What are you doing to leave a legacy? What are you doing when you wake up in the morning that's helping other people around the world? Not just lining your pockets and creating wealth for yourself. What are you doing that's going to be left behind once you're gone that other people can benefit from?

The book is one of those things. The book is a legacy that can be left behind and serve other people. So I'm very fortunate to have something like that that's going to be around for years to come.

Caren: I love that quote. One of the things that I teach the people that I work with is to give first and to come from the place of supporting. In fact, one of the questions that I ask everybody that I meet, and without even them knowing what I do, is, *how can I support you?*

11

And it's amazing the response that I get from almost everyone. *Wow! I can't believe you're not trying to sell me. You just want to know how to support me.* And they actually *say, I don't even know what to say right now,* which is kind of fun.

And they eventually come back, and I can support them. I can help them, because I want to show up first giving, because when they're ready for my services, who are they going to come to? Me.

Sohail: Well it's interesting you say that, because in my book I also mention how to connect with people, whether it's thought leaders, millionaires, or billionaires. And what you said hits the nail on the head.

Two things that I always teach my brokers or my clients when we go to a network and meet new people, the first question you should ask is an icebreaker question. That is, for example, if I saw you at an event, and I saw your nametag, I would say, *so Caren, tell me how did you get started doing hangouts?* Or how did you get started in terms of whatever you do?

That's a great icebreaker question, because people love it when other people are interested in them. We all love talking about ourselves. Another thing is we love people who are interested in us also. That really builds a big, strong connection.

And the second question to ask what you just said is *so Caren, how can I help you sell more of your product or service?* And that is exactly what you've just mentioned, which is spot on. So well done!

Caren: Well, thank you. Because it's a very cool thing. I actually get something from that. I feel really good about being able to help people. I feel very good about being able to support people.

In fact, we're doing this interview because I want to support your book launch, and I want people to understand the value that you bring to the table. If they might want to consider getting into a partnership with

12

someone, or a joint venture with someone, then you truly are THE Joint Venture Guy.

You are. And I don't even know what else to say, other than that you are THE Joint Venture Guy.

So this next question is going to kind of sound off somewhere, but -

Sohail: Okay.

Caren: - if you could spread passion dust anywhere in the world on anyone in the world, what would you hope to accomplish, and who would you spread it on?

Sohail: That's a really interesting question. I think you've got to look at where people are suffering at around the world and how we can help them.

I think all of us as entrepreneurs have certain skills that can be utilized. I think there are a lot of weird and crazy things happening around the world. A lot of things can be fixed. A lot of people can be helped. And it depends how we go about it.

But it comes back to joint venture partnering. Alone, we are strong. But together, forming partnerships with other people to deliver that, we're even stronger.

Caren: Exactly. I truly love that.

Now, we've been teasing people during this interview that we're going to send them somewhere to actually get a free copy of your book. All they have to pay is the shipping and handling. I think it's $7.99. Truly, that's giving, exactly along those same lines.

So where are we going to send people to do this?

Sohail: If you go to http://MillionDollarPartneringBook.com, you can go straight to the website and just register there. And you get the actual physical paperback copy of the book, which is worth $18 totally free; just pay the shipping and handling charge.

One of the main reasons we decided to do this was we wanted to get the book out to as many people as possible. I made a promise to Jay's family that I would keep his legacy alive through the book and I would get it out to as many people as possible. In the book is actually one of the last interviews that Jay did, and we did that together.

Also the book is everything I've ever done over the last 15 years to be successful at joint venture partnering. In the book there are certain, what should I say?, links for people to take this subject further. But there's no need to do that. Everything is provided in the book. And everything you need to be able to be successful is in the book.

I don't hold anything back. Everything I've ever done, I've ever taught, I've ever done myself, all my case studies are in the book.

That's at http://MillionDollarPartneringBook.com. So go there. For the next couple of days we're running a free promotion and you can pick the book up there.

Caren: I'm going to ask our readers, if you take advantage of this really amazing offer, go and leave a review on Amazon or leave a review somewhere in maybe Good Reads, somewhere to help get the cause out there.

It's wonderful that you are doing this for the Conrad Levinson family. I really truly appreciate that. So let's even get more visibility. Let's get some reviews out there. Even share it on your Facebook profile somewhere. So that we can support Sohail and the family of Jay Conrad Levinson to make sure that people that want to learn about this really can do it.

Any last thoughts Sohail, before we say goodbye?

Sohail: I think always follow your passion, do things that you enjoy, wake up in the morning and plan your day and just do the little things that you enjoy.

Most things in life don't require money, to be honest with you. Most people focus on that. But it just requires you to be able to live the life that you want and lead the life that you want. Always work for that and be persistent. I guarantee you will get there.

Caren: Awesome! Well, I want to thank you for being on the show today. And anything that I can do to support you. We will make sure that we connect.

So as always, we thank our readers. We know that you have lots of choices as to how you spend your time. We want to thank you for spending your time with us today. We will see you next time on *The Passion Point.*

Goodbye everyone.

LISA MONTALVA

APRIL 29, 2014

Caren: Hello everyone. Caren Glasser here. I'd like to welcome you to this episode of *The Passion Point*. This is the show where we interview Passionistas around the world who are doing something that they really love and making a living doing that.

Pretty cool!

Today we have another great guest. Her name is Lisa Montalva. She is out there on the East Coast, I am on the West Coast and through modern technology, we are sitting here together having this discussion.

Lisa, prior to founding the Women's Owned Business Club, she worked in Human Resources for 22 years. When she left that in 2006, she started her staffing firm and then her job board called the Job Matchers.

Eventually she continued into doing the Woman's Owned Business Club. And when you and I talk Lisa, about this organization, it's your giveback. So I'd like to welcome you to *The Passion Point*.

Lisa: Hi Caren. Thank you. Hello everybody.

Caren: So Lisa, I'd like to start with a definition for passion. According to *Webster's Dictionary*, it says that *passion is an intense driving or overmastering feeling or conviction*. Does that resonate with you? Or how would you describe passion?

Lisa: Absolutely. The Woman Owned Business Club is now my passion and my partner's passion. It's just this incredible feeling. Every time I speak to them, I go to bed happy and I wake up happy. Not that I didn't do that in my other career, but it's just a different feeling.

I get to speak to amazing women every day, and we did this to inspire other women. But in fact, they're inspiring us. It's just the most amazing, wonderful thing. Back in my day in Manhattan, I had friend philanthropists they'd say, *oh my goodness, it's so nice to do this and give back.* And I'd be, clip-clopping with my Manolo Blahniks down the street thinking, *it's not real.* And it is.

Until you actually feel it in your bones, you don't know. This is our passion now. We're very, very lucky.

Caren: I love that definition, because it is a feeling. It is definitely something that just comes over you when you know you're doing something that you're meant to do.

So let's talk about you, Lisa. Let's talk about how you became the woman that you are today. Let's go way, way back. When did you know that you wanted to help people and to be a service to people?

Lisa: Well, it didn't really start until after the Job Matchers launched, and I found it very disheartening that after spending $300K on getting my first company up and running, there was no real help out there. I really didn't understand why.

In every organization I joined, whatever the case may be, everyone just had their hand out, which is fine. I understand that. But no one was willing to actually say, or give me any advice or anything like that. Even though I came from Human Resources, and I was considered - I hate to use this - a big shot. I really came out with a big ego and thinking it was going to be really, really easy, because I was Lisa Montalva - it didn't work out that way.

So I knew something had to be done, but I didn't know what. I worked the Job Matchers, and after just not even a business model of what I thought should be done, we worked it. I worked it. In that term, when I started Job Matchers, I met my partner Christine Lynch. We're just in sync with each other.

I told her about the Women's Owned Business Club and what I wanted to do and we worked it together. But we worked on Job Matchers first. That was our first goal. Now we have 32 million people coming to our job board every month.

So since that worked, we went to the Gourmet Mom, which is my recipe website. I had written a cookbook before meeting Christine. We built the recipe website and now we have about four million people coming to the Gourmet Mom. We're turning that into an online magazine as well because we want to help all the foodies out there.

We're going to be doing the same thing we do with the Women Owned Business Club and having them submit their recipes. We'll promote them every day.

We both built a huge base just on LinkedIn alone. I have 45 million direct connections on LinkedIn.

Caren: I'm exhausted. Lisa, I'm exhausted.

Lisa: Well, people say that, but you know what? We work 17 hours a day sometimes. At least we used to. I'm building and it's not just about picking people. It's actually going in and looking at people and connecting with people and seeing if they're a right fit.

You don't just want to send your information to people who don't want it. To me, that's useless. I see people doing it just on Facebook alone. All they do is promote their stuff. You have to get an audience, the right audience. It's just not working.

So the Women Owned Business Club came into being. We're doing phenomenal. I think it's like 430 members in two years. Since we built that, we're continuously building new platforms. We built the WOBC magazine, which we have a subscribed audience of 10 million. So it's just huge, huge numbers. It's like unfathomable how we have all these people, but it's - it's just thousands of people coming to the website, both of them, the magazine or the website, there's thousands of people, tens of thousands of page views.

What we're doing is working and we want to help other people, because they're basically renting our space at only $69 a year to join. We promote them. We give them 12,440 posts a year and that's just for their business. If they write articles, it's 12,440 posts for each article.

It's a huge amount of work. We're giving free e-courses. It's just so much we want to give, because I believe in value. I was trapped into it too. People asked me to join their things, but they do nothing for you. Not that they don't have value, but they don't have the value that we want to give.

We want to teach. We want to help. We want to inspire. We want to talk these ladies off the bridge, because sometimes they're on the bridge, because they don't know what to do. And there's hard times out there for some people. I would say a good portion of the people out there are struggling.

Caren: Right. Well that leads me into my next question. What do you tell people that have lost their passion or have lost their way and they just don't know what to do next? Because I agree with you. There are more people out there that are unhappy, that are frustrated, that really feel like there's no hope than there are people that feel that there is hope.

What do you tell these people?

Lisa: A lot of times Christie and I talk to these people and we give the information. We give them insight about either their website or just certain things, even how they're promoting themselves. Once we tell them these certain little things, they're just happy that we even took the time to do that for them. And that helps them.

I tell them all the time, because some people go into business and they think in three months they're going to make money. You have to have patience. It's terrible when you probably need food. You need to pay your electrical bill. I understand that, but go slow and steady. That is our motto, me and Christie. Go slow and steady, maintain, and be patient.

That is the biggest thing that people want. They want immediate results. I get immediate gratification. I'm big on that. But it doesn't work in this type of business. It just doesn't, especially now with the internet.

Caren: Exactly. And would you agree that you need to grow your tribe? I mean, you need to build your raving fans, and you need to give-give-give-give before you ask for something?

Lisa: That's exactly right. We give a lot of stuff. Our resources, what we give, is huge amounts of money. But that's another thing, I tell entrepreneurs all the time, they're going to have to give a lot away for free to brand themselves. It's just, you have to build those relationships and trust, and that's just the name of the game now.

Caren: Yeah, so I'm actually Facebook stalking you, because what you're doing is working. There is no question it's working.

I see multiple posts and things that come out from you constantly promoting other people. And I am sure that you get approached by a gazillion people.

Lisa: Yeah.

Caren: What can you do for me? Right.

Lisa: Well yeah. It's funny. And I hate to sound like this, but you can't imagine the amount of phone calls every single day, *we're going to offer you this.* And I find it, I can't say insulting, because I understand, because we were there too. But me and Christie, we worked our butts off and now they want to jump on our back.

I don't think so.

I don't think so.

No. Especially when - no. I'm sorry. It's very bothersome. We've come across a lot of wonderful people, and they have organizations. We're going to help those people and we're going to do what we can.

Caren: But those numbers are pretty incredible. When I first was reading about you, I was looking at the visibility that you have and your magazine subscriptions and your site views. Very few people can boast about that.

Lisa: People said I did it backwards and I felt I didn't. I was building my audience before I actually had the products. I would send out emails and say, this is what it's going to do. And that's how I built my audience.

I built my audience first before I had the product. It's certainly not the way it's done, but that's the way I did it.

Caren: One might say that you were doing research, R&D, right?

Lisa: Yeah, because it's informational. I was saying, is this going to work? And it did for us. It really, really did. That's how we have this huge audience.

People are just, they're happy with what we do. It's nice. We can't guarantee everyone's going to make a million in sales, but we increase search visibility. Every time you put a post on the internet, it goes into the search engines. And that's what you need.

We want you to be able to put your name or life coach or something like that. More than 99% of the time it's going to be attached to Woman Owned Business Club. And that's really important.

Our directories are open. Just the directory today, I mean, we have over 41-42K page views today. I mean, that's a day! Just page views of people looking at the directory. Having an open directory is very important.

We do block out the email address and their phone numbers, only because of the spam, and we don't want that. If they really are interested in them, they can go find them. They can go to their Facebook, their Twitter, their Pinterest, their website and they can contact them.

Those are real results. Those are real people that are really interested in them.

Caren: Well I think that's great, because when we get to the end, which we're nowhere near our conversation at the end, we will give people the link to actually get in touch with the Women Owned Business Club, how they can join. You said it before, the price point on your club is ridiculous, quite frankly.

Lisa: Some people do call me and they'll say we've been watching you forever. Most of the people don't think we're real, because we charge so little. There's that yin and yang. Do you charge a lot of money?

I just don't believe in that. I'd rather charge less and have that value. But some people are addicted to - *oh no, it must be $995 for it to be really good.* And no. That's not the way it has to be.

Caren: So you're an anomaly, I only wish that, and I'm sure you are an example to others who want to be of service and who want to show up in a way that's - I hate the word authentic, but I'm going to use it today. You're showing up.

Lisa: Yeah, no definitely we show up. It's funny, when they call, they're like, *we can't believe we got you or we got Christie on the phone. How is this possible?*

Because our organization is about being a family. I mean, this is what happened when I called another organization I belong to. I didn't call them today. I called them last Wednesday. I only get a phone call today.

And I don't understand. It's hundreds of dollars to belong to this organization that I've belonged to for years, and they don't call me back. They call me back and they told me that someone else had to call me back. I just don't get that.

Me and Christie, when we're on the phone, we will work with that person. If they have a question or a problem, we'll figure it out at that moment. We're not going to ask you to call back. We're going to work. And that is very important to people, I think.

Caren: Imagine that! A live person on the other end answering the phone!

Lisa: They call and they're like, *hello?* I'm like, *hello.*

I'm looking for Lisa Montalva. Is it possible I could leave her a voice mail? I said, *you have her. You can speak to her.*

They're like, *we're speaking to you?* I'm like *yeah, you're speaking to me.*

Caren: But doesn't that speak volumes to what people are used to?

Lisa: Absolutely. We're used to that. I get that all the time. Call the bank, you can't even get a live person. It drives me crazy.

Caren: Again, the devil's in the follow up. So if somebody calls you and they don't return the call. That makes me crazy.

Lisa: Christie and I are crazy about that. Everyone can reach us through a phone call, email, Facebook. We have many, many different outlets. And we're on top of it. Immediately someone is called back.

If it's within the hour, that would be the most amount of time that is a lag.

Caren: So let's talk a little bit outside of this right now. I love quotes. I love to start my day and in the middle of the day and at the end of the day find something that speaks to me so that it kind of pushes me through the rest of the day.

Today I picked a quote that I'd like to share with you and hopefully you'll have a quote that you can share with us. The quote today says, *in life change is inevitable. In business, change is vital.* And that was written by Warren G. Bennis. What do you think about that?

Lisa: That's great. That's a really great quote.

I'm very big on the quotes. I try to pick things that whether I write them or I pick them out to put on my page, I want people to know that I'm a real person and Christie's a real person. We're women. We have struggles. We have family. We have this. We want people to see us as real people.

I try every morning to inspire somebody, make them understand that they're not alone. We're here. I always say, whether you're a friend, a fan, a follower, whatever you are, there's hope. That is our thing every single day. We're just trying to inspire them and say, get up! It's okay. You can do it. It's okay that you failed too.

Failing is okay. A lot of people don't want to do that. Fight it and fail, with the Job Matchers. I shouldn't say it failed. But it was up and down and spending so much money and really didn't know what to do. If I made a mistake leaving my career in Manhattan.

Because I left. I quit my job. So thank God I did, because the Woman Owned Business Club wouldn't be here. It's my love. It's our baby. This is what we do. This is like our child. Me and Christie are like married forever now, you know. This is it! This is our baby.

Caren: So what quote can you share with us that maybe you shared today on social media?

Lisa: I don't know. I'm all mixed up in my head. I don't know what to say exactly. I'm always about *think big, dream big*. That's an important one to me. And maybe it's just widespread.

But I want people, to stop talking about thinking outside the box. There's no box. There's no box, just think and do, and there's no box. So I really can't give you an exact quote. I'm sorry.

Caren: No-no, that's perfect actually though. It's inspirational and it's motivational and it doesn't have to be. That's your quote. So we'll attribute that to you.

So you play on social media obviously. You play on Facebook and LinkedIn. Where else are you playing?

Lisa: We play on Twitter. LinkedIn, yes. LinkedIn, Twitter, Facebook, Google+. I have five of them.

Caren: Are you on Pinterest at all?

Lisa: Yes, Pinterest too. Oh yeah, we're there, all day. I really need more arms. I have seven computers on my desk. We do have staff, but yeah, it's a little bit exhausting, but it's fun too. You can get really addicted.

My favorite really is Pinterest and Facebook, only because they're very visual. Twitter is very exhausting. You really have to be on that. And I really focus on one day of the week I come on that.

I mean, every day I answer back. I make sure that, we have a new follower. And I acknowledge them. I think it's very important to acknowledge the people who have liked you. If it's okay, return the favor. I always give them a shout out. That kind of stuff is important.

But social media, you have to be in it. You really, really have to be in it. I would suggest these people out there, if you don't have a huge staff or you can't handle it, just try one or two of them. Don't try to overwhelm yourself, because that's silly. Build your audience on one, Facebook or what have you. Or else you'll fail, unfortunately. It won't work.

Caren: I agree. I think one of the reasons that a lot of people don't get involved in social media is they get so overwhelmed, because somebody told them somewhere you can't just do Facebook. You have to be on Twitter and you have to be on Pinterest. You have to be on Google+.

Lisa: We have a lot of members, like oh my goodness, we don't have this or that. You don't have to. If you just want to brand your website, that's perfectly fine. You don't have to.

But we always suggest one or two of them. And we teach them. And we tell them, yes, it's definitely exhausting. I wake up in the middle of the night just thinking about Twitter and all night, it's like crazy. Our brains, how they are now. But yeah, thinking about posts and what I have to do and what doesn't have to be done.

Caren: I have a question for you, because you mentioned something about following people on Twitter. Do you manually follow them? Or do you have an auto response? Are you actually going in there?

Lisa: No, because we get too many. Last week, I just blocked probably 3000 people because they were just posting. They follow you and then they want to use your name. And they sell, I'm not going to say junk, but

27

a lot of them are spammers out there. They're selling Twitter followers. We don't want that on our pages.

I want it to be good content. Our content is all about our members. So no, it's absolutely manual. We do not auto follow.

Caren: I am even more impressed with you right now than I was before.

Lisa: It's a lot of work. I kept thinking all day, oh my God, I have to talk to Caren at seven o'clock. I'm so tired. But it's fine. I'm good. I'm happy that we got to do this.

Caren: Well I'm happy too. This is going to be a silly question, but maybe not so silly. If you could spread passion dust anywhere around the world, who would you spread it on and what would you hope to accomplish?

Lisa: Oh my goodness, passion dust! I guess, honestly, because I'm a single mom - I mean, my kids are 20 and 26 now, but I would sprinkle the dust on the single mothers who feel lost and they have to rebuild their lives. When their husbands are not paying them, I would sprinkle it on them and say, *you have the power sweetheart. And you're going to do it*, and that's where I would give it.

Absolutely, that's where I would give it.

Caren: So do you have a song that you're passionate about?

Lisa: A song? No, not really. I mean, there's - I don't know. I mean, I have Sirius in my truck and I sing Aretha Franklin. I'm big country. I love country music. It's really deep.

Caren: I'm with you on that one. One of my favorite songs is *Hell Yeah!* You know, the *Redneck Woman*. That's my favorite song. So I'm a country girl as well, we have that in common.

Do you have a guilty passion?

Lisa: I do. From last night until this morning, I ate a box of Milano cookies. And I'm like, thank God I went to the gym, because you forget. I keep going to the drawer, and I'm like *I ate one,* and *I ate two,* and then I'm like, *they're all gone. What did I do? I ate them.* So just another extra mile I've got go on the bike or something.

I've been trying not to eat sugar during the week, because I've been feeling sick, because I'm a sugar junkie. I would rather eat a cake for dinner than have something else, but I've been doing much better. I've usually been trying really hard, like Saturdays are my cupcake days. Such a loser!

But that's my big thing. I have a cupcake on a Saturday night.

Caren: So Lisa, if people want to get in touch with you, if they want to find out more about the Women Owned Business Club or more about your Job Matchers or maybe get onto the board because they're looking for a job, can you give us some sites to the go to? And how do we get in touch with you?

Lisa: Sure. The Job Matchers is http://TheJobMatchers.com. And the Women Owned Business Club, you can go to http://WOBC.info. That's the shorter link. All our information is there. They can contact us.

Just Google my name and you'll be able to find me. We're on Facebook. The Women Owned Business Club. It's very easy to find us. All the information is there to join. They want to email us, we'll get back to them.

Caren: That's fabulous. And I know they can check you out as well on Facebook. You have fan pages and all sorts of cool stuff on Pinterest. I encourage our listeners to go to check this out, because she is the real deal. Lisa, you are the real deal. And I'm just so happy that we had a chance to meet. For me to be able to introduce you to my network out there so that they can come and see what you're doing.

Lisa: Thank you so much. I couldn't have done this without my partner. I have to give her kudos. Christine Lynch. She's the best. It's both of us. She's amazing!

Caren: So a shout out to Christine Lynch as well. You have the information how to get in touch with both Lisa and Christine and the Women Owned Business Club, everything.

I encourage you to reach out and just touch.

Just do it!

Take action today. Just do it.

So Lisa, any last parting comments you'd like to say before we say goodbye?

Lisa: Thank you so much Caren. It was lovely talking to you. I love speaking about what we do. And yeah, I urge the women if they need help, they want to join, that's fine. If they don't, that's fine too, we're here to help. If anyone has a question, we're more than happy to help any of the women out there who just have a question and don't know where to go or what to start. Any kind of question they have, and that's fine.

Caren: Well, thank you so much, and I just want to thank our audience We know that you have a choice every single day as to how you spend your time. We are honored that you chose to spend it with us today.

As always, have a great week. We'll see you next week on the next episode of *The Passion Point*. Goodbye everyone.

FORD SAEKS

SEPTEMBER 8, 2014

Caren: Hello everyone. Caren Glasser here from *The Passion Point*. This is the show where we interview Passionistas from around the world who are following their passion and making a living doing what they love.

Today we have Ford Saeks with us. He's an entrepreneur since birth, when he tried to sell tickets to his kindergarten class for recess. Imagine that!

He is now positioned as one of America's top marketing mentors. Saeks' sales producing, profit-generating solutions help people reach success in new and existing business ventures.

He built his first business at 16. I want to hear all about that Ford, because that's got to be pretty incredible, and pretty motivational for our teenagers that will be reading this as well. He's labeled a "true entrepreneur." His patented products have sold millions and sell worldwide through retail stores, mail order catalogs, mass merchants, and electronic retailers.

He took risks, he used his instincts, and he figured out what works in a highly competitive marketplace. Today he is focused on his company called Prime Concepts. We're going to be talking about that today as well.

So I'd like to introduce Ford to our interview. Come on Ford. How are you doing today?

Ford: I'm doing great. Thanks so much for having me. I'm happy to be here and happy to share some great tips and strategies.

Caren: Awesome! That is great, because you have quite the journey that you've been on, and I know that people are going to want to hear what you have to say.

We always start our show with a definition of passion. According to *Webster's Dictionary*, it's an *intense, driving, or overmastering feeling or conviction.* That's what *Webster's* says. What does Ford say? What's passion?

Ford: I would say that's pretty close. I know that when I first started my first business at 15 years old, I was certainly more passionate than experienced or educated. I think that if I had to choose, I think that passion's a primary, dominant factor in everything.

In fact, when I go to hire people for my company, I would rather find passion and enthusiasm. I can teach someone the skills, but I can't teach someone the passion and the enthusiasm.

Caren: That is such a valid point. That is so true. You can't teach it. It's got to come from within.

So what is your view on passion, and how has it effected what you have done? I mean, we talked about the fact in kindergarten you were selling tickets. I mean, that's a little unusual. Tell us a little about that and how maybe it formulated who you became today.

Ford: I think that passion and underlying power started when I was in the projects. I moved into the housing projects in North Minneapolis at the age of 12.

At 12 years old, I moved out. I was on my own. I was in foster care. I went into the projects because I could pay $17 a month for government housing, and I could live.

After about three years of living in the projects and still going to grade school and then junior high, I wanted to figure out a way to make money other than how everybody in my neighborhood was making money. I decided I would start a painting company, because when I was in detention centers, anytime I would swear or cuss Caren, as punishment they would make me paint.

I became a good little painter. That first little year at age 15, I started a painting company. I can certainly go into more of those details, but it was the passion to change my life. It was the passion to move away from what I didn't want, towards what I did want. I kind of leapt and grew my wings on the way down.

I didn't exactly know what I was going to do, but I knew I didn't want what I was doing. I was passionate to make a difference and that's what drove me to make that difference.

Caren: What would be your advice to kids today that are in foster care? That's something I didn't know about you.

What would you tell young people that find themselves in a situation that you found yourself? Where did you find the strength to pull yourself up and how do you encourage other youth to do the same thing?

Ford: It all starts with a success library. You have to manage what you put in your mind. What you put in is what you get out. If you spend your time watching TV or doing things that are destructive or things that are not going to help you, you're not going to take advantage of the ideas that come into your presence.

At 15 years old, I was motivated. I didn't have any money. I wanted my life to be different. I wanted the things that other people have. In order to do that, I had to be willing to do the things that other people wouldn't do.

I went to my friends in shop class, and I made up some flyers that said, Saeks' painting and light construction. It said light construction because I didn't have any construction experience. I put up some flyers around town. Finally after about two weeks, I got a voice message on my old reel-to-reel answering machine, which was back in the mid-'70s.

I was all excited. But then Caren, I thought, *holy crap! I don't own a paintbrush! I have nothing. I have no experience. What do I do?*

I had a message from someone who wanted me to do the proposal. I said, I know what I can do. I'll go to the local paint store, because they know how to do this. So I went to the paint store, walked up to the counter, talked to the manager, and said, *Sir, I just started this painting company. Could you please help me?*

He took a look at me, and said, *get the heck out of here.* Now, I didn't realize at the time. I had long hair, an army jacket, a 9 mm. I didn't exactly look like a business owner. He went ahead and gave me all the instructions I needed. He went over to the paint, grabbed a brush, started speckling me with paint. So now I've got paint all over me and he gave me a clipboard, a calculator, and instructions, and I was off to the house.

Do you still want to hear the rest of the story?

34

Caren: Yes, I do, actually, because would you say that was your first mentor?

Ford: I would say the first mentor was probably a Denis Waitley tape on the *Psychology of Winning*, because that was the first thing that expanded my mind to let go of my past and that things could be different. That was probably the turning point that motivated me to do that.

When I went to the house, I knocked on the door, I went through the house, and the gentlemen pointed at the ceilings. He said, *I want the ceiling fans fixed, the ceilings around the ceiling fans. I want the windows glazed. I want flat-based paint here and oil-based paint here.* And I am way overwhelmed at this point, but I'm writing it all down, and I'm thinking, *oh my goodness, how can I get the heck out of here?*

I took all the notes. And I'm thinking *paint is paint. What's this semi-gloss and eggshell and flat and oil?* I knew nothing. But I told him I had to go back to my office to prepare the proposal. Went back to the paint store, told the gentlemen what I needed. He helped me calculate all the materials and everything I would need.

Back to the house I went. Knocked on the door. The door swings open. This time the man's wife is standing there looking right at me. She takes one look at me and steps right behind her husband.

I'm thinking, *oh this isn't going to go well.* I gave her the proposal. I said, *here's the proposal to paint the inside of your house. It's $1025. I need 50% up front and 50% on completion of the job.*

She took a look at me, took a look at the proposal, and said, *do you have any experience?*

Well this is a critical point in my business, because I'm trying to decide, *do I tell them I repainted the whole North Wing of the Huntington County Detention Center?* Or do I tell them what I told them? What I said is *if you're not 100% satisfied with the job, you don't have to pay.*

She said, *honey, write him a check.* I got that check for $525, which at that time was more than I made in two months. I looked at this check. And I said, *wow! I'm going to learn how to do this as an entrepreneur.* That actually created the passion to move forward. That first year in business, I had three crews working for me. They were 40 years old and I generated $35K in sales.

Now that doesn't sound like a lot right now, but let me do the math. In equivalence, it's $175K worth of income. So at 15, I made $175K income.

The problem is, when you give a kid from the projects $35K, they spend $36K. I had to learn about cash flow and management and some of those other things that came later. But that's what started my business. That's what got me on the line of entrepreneurship.

Caren: Oh gosh. That is a great story! So basically: say yes and figure it out later. Right?

Ford: Well, you know, you still want to do the best you can at making sure that you have a plan or a direction to go. I mean, you don't want to spend your time running east looking for a sunset. You have to still go in the right direction.

Caren: Absolutely.

So after you started this paint company and you started to make some real money, where did you go from there?

Ford: Well the painting company lasted for a few years. Then I moved because I was a speed skater in Minnesota. I was fast enough to be awarded a term at the Olympic training center.

A friend of mine, we were going out to the Olympic training center as resident athletes in 1979, which is a long time ago, I know. We drove from Minneapolis south to Kansas City and when we got to Kansas City, I was 18 years old. He said, *I know a girl in Wichita. We can go down and spend some time there.* So we came to Wichita, Kansas and we ran out of money. The USA boycotted the '80 Olympics and I stayed.

Ever since then, people have said, *why do you live in Wichita, Kansas?* And what I would tell them is as a professional, speaker, author, and expert, I travel around the world, so it's a really nice place to come back to. There's no traffic. I can get where I want. The cost of living is good. And of course, I have my company here with all my employees. So it's really worked out well.

Caren: So how did Prime Concepts come about? And tell us a little bit about what it is actually and how did it come about?

Ford: Well Prime Concepts is an integrated marketing company that helps people attract and keep their customers. We do that through integrated marketing campaigns, internet marketing, publicity, all different types of lead magnets, traffic and conversions.

Where it came from, I have to back up. After the paint company I had several other companies and then I was racing bicycles professionally. I invented a bike rack that goes from floor to ceiling. You've probably seen it on TV. It's been on a lot of shows and it's just a pull system.

When I first came up with that Caren, people told me it would never sell. Everybody I showed it to, including so-called marketing experts, said you will never sell it. Why would somebody pay $99-$189 for something that they can get a hook for $0.99?

Well 50 million in retail sales later, it was selling quite well. I sold the company. It was a sporting goods company. After I did that, people would come to me and they would say, how do you sell to Wal-Mart? How do you invent a product? How do you patent a product? How do you get 4K dealers? How do you sell to catalogs? How do you do trade shows?

I started that first year after I sold my sporting goods company to realize that I really have another business, and that was teaching people how to do what I had done. That was the foundation of Prime Concepts. Since that time, we've sold millions of products. We're responsible for over one billion in sales for our clients.

Caren: I know you have television shows. Tell us a little bit about that.

Ford: Well certainly. As an entrepreneur, as a marketer, one of the things you want to do is get more exposure. Just like what we're doing today. I'm a guest on your show. I'm getting exposed to people who don't know me.

Now in this case, it's an internet show. It's from your website, and it's a Google hangout, but it's still exposure. More people get to know me, they get to know my name.

I didn't create any fancy giveaway or lead magnet today to say all your readers can go to Prime Concepts and get something special. I basically am just here to suggest today to get more exposure and then to help your readers out, to give back, because a lot of people over the years have given to me.

I think the key with the television, the actual broadcast television, it's the same purpose. I identified the market that I wanted to reach, I looked for ways to be visible, because most people believe that they're spending all this time and they're worried about being over-exposed, when in reality they're probably obscure and nobody even knows who they are.

I guarantee that even though I've had TV shows and I've been on TV, nobody knows who I am. I'm not a super, super star. I'm known in my circles. I'm known in my areas. But not everywhere. So the TV, what that does is it gives me social proof and credibility so that when I go to sell my speaking engagements they say, *yes, this guy's a credible author, expert, and business leader. Let's bring him in.*

Caren: You're so right. That's exactly why I do my shows. I have a couple of shows. It's internet TV, but it's TV, and we do podcasts and stuff.

I think that a lot of business owners miss the boat on this, because they seem to think that they're in their own little circle. It must be the whole world who knows them, even though it's just their own little circle. I really respect what you just said. I do believe that a lot of people know who you are, Ford. But it is truly that. And I do think that business owners are missing the boat.

What do you think about that? Are they missing the boat in marketing themselves like that?

Ford: They absolutely are missing the boat. Whether they're using Google Hangouts like we're doing and doing a live broadcast or whether they're just doing YouTube videos.

Here's the deal. In 2014, like we are now, and almost 2015, there's never been a time in history where anybody with a webcam and a laptop can establish their authority.

I mean, look at the TV nowadays. Any show you watch, they're going to say, go to our website and vote. I don't care if it's *American Idol* or *America's Got Talent* or *Big Brother*. Whatever the show is, there's always some type of polling interaction.

The broadcast medium has changed. It's no longer just internet or just TV. It's actually merged. A lot of people see it now. Even the TV set is connected and you can do all these things. Our broadcast today can get found on a TV set.

It's changing. So business owners today are missing the boat in establishing their footprint.

Even if they're a local business - I speak to a lot of franchise organizations to help them grow their business. Now when I work for franchise organizations, most of them are local, because it's a franchise. They're trying to drive foot traffic into a store or to buy products and services. Well they still can benefit from leveraging a YouTube channel, leveraging video marketing, leveraging shows, whether it's a how-to show like what we're doing, a tip show, a demo.

It doesn't matter what kind of store. I was working with a store in Florida, and I told them. You could do a weekly show on grilling. You have 250 products. You could take one product off the shelf and do a show about it, do a product or recipes or cooking or featured this. For a landscaping company I said, why aren't you doing before and afters? Why aren't you going and talking about a landscape and showing your before and afters and using video?

Caren: Absolutely. I do a lot of stuff with digital assets and digital footprints as well. One of the things that we tell business owners is what are those 10 questions that people always ask you.

Go create 10 little videos on YouTube that answer those questions. Put them out there and let them work for you rather than you working for them. When somebody asks you one of those questions, send them over to one of those videos. It's all about creating that digital asset, because if you're not out there, you're not going to be found.

Where do people go to find you right now? They're going to go to Google, right? They're going to research marketing, and you're going to show up. So if you're not on the web, you're not going to be found.

Ford: I think it's about two things: findability and usability. When it comes to findability, you talked about creating those top 10 videos and getting them labeled. It's not just create the videos. I worked with a client this morning. We were on the phone doing a business accelerator call. They had a lot of videos. She's an expert past LPGA - I might have the initials wrong, but from Cindy Miller Golf. You guys can look this up.

Anyway, I was working with her and she has all these videos, but none of them have keywords. So even though she had the content, she didn't title them properly. She didn't put the tags in properly. She didn't distribute them properly. Even though she took all this time to create this video content, keywords drive traffic. So findability is key.

And if I could just toss in one more note, for those people that are hopefully taking notes. I think it was Ben Franklin or someone who said go get a $0.10 pencil and write down some million dollar ideas. So if you're taking notes, I would just tell you and all your readers this: if you want to get traffic to your website, there's only three ways to do it. Just three ways.

You can create it, you can borrow it, or you can buy it.

Under create it, there's blogging and article marketing and the inbound marketing and social media marketing - LinkedIn, Facebook, Twitter, Google+, Instagram, whatever. And the new ones that haven't even been invented yet. You can create it by using your content.

You can borrow it by finding people who reach the same market you do and sharing content, like I'm doing today with you. I'm going to share this Google hangout with my market. You're going to share it with yours. We're going to both share each other. It's worked. We spend time together. It's a great deal. So it's borrowing the influence of another person.

Or you can pay for it. So you can create it, borrow it, or buy it.

Caren: I love that. That's awesome. And yes, I mean, I left out the SEO and the keywords and all that. The other thing that I think people forget is there's no call to action in their videos.

41

So here they are, they have a video, they're talking about whatever it is that they do. And maybe they did keyword. But there's no way to reach them, because they didn't put a call to action. What do you think about that?

Ford: I think you've been a little fly on my wall, because that's the biggest thing I tell all my clients. I look at the flow of their marketing messages and I look for headlines, sub-heads, magic stories, benefits, features, trial close, social proof, credibility, and above all - call to action.

If they forget everything, they need a headline and a call to action. Often they forget that call to action. What's their call to action? Now my call to action for anybody here watching this today would be go to YouTube and subscribe to my Prime Concepts YouTube channel. Follow me on Facebook. You can Google my name. You can easily find out who I am.

Obviously if you're a meeting planner, I would say hire me to bring me in. But I believe in one single call to action and that is share something of value. If you found this valuable, share it. I'm sure there are share buttons below. Share this video with other people that you know need to hear this message today.

Caren: That's awesome and so right on point. I'm glad we agree. What can you tell somebody as an adult, let's say - I like to call accidental entrepreneurs. People who have lost their jobs and they find themselves nowhere and they can't find a job because the job market is so bad. Now they become an entrepreneur, because it sounds better than I'm unemployed.

What do you tell people who have lost their job, they've lost their way, they don't know what their passion is, what do you tell them, or how do you help them get their mojo back?

Ford: I would say a couple of things. One, there's no free cheese in the mousetrap. Two, I would say there's no such thing as a money problem, only an idea problem. If you want to earn more money, whether it's through an entrepreneur or going back and getting a job at a regular career, you have to think about how you can add value.

Now I know this is going to irritate a lot of people because they want to be victims and whiners and say, *no - it's the economy. It's my boss who's an idiot.*

It's not. I got news for you. There's no shortage of success out there. If you have more success Caren, it doesn't take away from my success. It's not that kind of thing. There's never-ending success.

Now, have I had my challenges? Of course I have! I've had 17 different companies. I've never gone bankrupt. Three of them went multi-million. The rest of them I either sold or let go of because they weren't positive.

So my point is you have to go keep going. What would I tell those people? I would say, quit whining, get off your butt, and make a list of all the things you like to do. More importantly, ask yourself this question - what problems do I solve that people are willing to pay to make go away? What are you good at that people are willing to pay for?

I mean, I have my pool cleaned, my hot tub cleaned, my house cleaned. I have meals cooked for me. I have my car picked up and cleaned. I have my dry cleaning picked up and cleaned. I have two executive assistants. That costs a lot of money.

I make good money, don't get me wrong. But I would rather pay them to do that and go read a book and do something where I can add more value. So the question I would ask is: what problems do you solve that people will pay to make go away? Is what you're doing the highest and best use of your time?

43

If you're an accidental entrepreneur and you're unemployed and you're looking for something to do, first find something that's lifestyle friendly, that you're passionate about, and then take massive action. And really, that's two things.

With YouTube nowadays Caren, and you know this, there's no shortage of answers. Everything's at our fingertips. This isn't like it was 20 years ago. If I don't know how to do something go to YouTube and type it in. It doesn't matter what it is, there's probably going to be some expert like you or me that's put 10-15 videos up and in an afternoon you can get all your questions answered.

How to get a career here or there, how to start a new business, all that information is out there. Now obviously you have to sift through it and that's one of the reasons where companies like yours and mine excel. Because sure, people could learn what you and I are teaching for free. But they'll also pay a premium amount because they don't have to struggle to figure out what worked and what didn't. They can go straight to the experts like us and get the answers.

Caren: Great advice. I'm all about quotes. I love quotes. I try to find a quote to get my day started. Today I'm going to tell you one of my favorite quotes and maybe you have a quote that you'd like to share with our readers as well.

Today's quote is, and this was written by Charles Schwab, *a person can succeed at almost anything for which they have unlimited enthusiasm.* What do you think?

Ford: I think that's a great quote. I actually have an app that comes on my phone every day. This one just happens to be called FitOne. The quote of today is *the difficult is that which can be done immediately. The impossible takes them longer.*

I didn't know what the quote would be today. I just happened to pull it up and click it. But I encourage everyone to create a success library where they're filling themselves with positive information.

44

I'm not talking about the Secret manifesto. You can read *The Secret* every single day of your life. Nothing's going to change, unless you take action.

Now I know - a lot of those people on *The Secret* are friends. I have to be careful. I know a lot of them, but my point is you still have to take action. At the end of the day just ask yourself, how much action did you really take?

It's so funny. I work with a lot of people who are in sales and a lot of speakers even that are in sales. It's funny because they always call me. How do you get more speaking engagements? How do you get more bookings? How do you do this? I always ask them, how much time are you spending eye to eye, face to face, toe to toe with your prospects? Are you sending out emails? Are you calling? Are you on LinkedIn? Are you prospecting?

Most of them aren't doing anything. They're just sitting back waiting for the phone to ring. I think most people, including me, are delusional about how much time they really spend marketing and unfortunately everybody's involved in marketing. I don't care if you have 100 people in your company, 100 people are involved in marketing.

That's my two cents. I don't have a particular quote other than to make sure that you're listening, watching, or reading something that interests you on your topic or desires every day, even if it's 15 minutes. Spend 15 minutes. Listen to something in the car on the way to work.

I use Audible. I have a whole list of books. I've got a success library, and that's just one my current one. So I always make sure that I have two books with me on the road. The one, the book I'm reading, and the other, the book I'm writing.

Caren: I love that! So that was my next question. Can you give us two of your favorite books that you believe everyone should have on their shelf?

Ford: Well it really depends on the topic area. I'm going to name a few and then tell you: If you have a problem with prosperity, if any time that Caren or I have talked about money or amounts, and you have belief systems about money all the how-to books in the world are not going to help you. You've got to get your prosperity fixed first.

I would obviously recommend anything by Randy Gage, partly because I'm the publisher and I publish all of his products. But partly because they are really good products to help you as a critical thinker, to think differently. Even if you don't agree with everything that he says, it's certainly a way to get you to think differently.

Any author on prosperity, there's a million gurus out there, people that can help you. I would say prosperity first. Then I would say there's a great book called Darren Hardy called *The Compound Effect*.

Caren: Awesome book.

Ford: It's a great book. Obviously the old greats. I've got Napoleon Hill's *The Law of Success*, which is an old book from the '50s. It's the same things regurgitated. So for those of you experts - I'm just going to do a side note.

I was at this event last weekend in Orlando. There were all these 20-something entrepreneurs in the room. There were a couple 30 year olds. And here I am, I'm 53. I'm an old fart.

I'm watching these guys talk about marketing. They're going, yeah, I did this thing. It's called split testing, where you do one headline and you do another. I'm thinking, I'*m an old direct response mail guy. I used to mail one million pieces a month. They think that they've reinvented direct mail because it's the internet.*

The point I'm making is there's really no new information out there. It's really your story in it. It's the same with your business. A lot of businesses think they're a commodity, but they're not. I don't care if it's insurance, real estate, dentistry, you still have to have a unique selling proposition, something that makes you stand out from the competition.

Caren: I also believe that you have to create that relationship. People are not going to buy from you if they don't have that relationship. They don't know, like, and trust you. It's that old cliché saying, but they have to get to know you.

Have you read Jeff Olsen's *The Slight Edge*?

Ford: No, I haven't read that book. I will write that one down to add it to my library.

Caren: That's actually talking about going towards your goals in short incremental steps. It's a great book for the library and for our readers as well.

I have one more question for you Ford. We could go on for hours. I'm fascinated just by what you're talking about, and I so totally agree with what you're saying.

The question is this: if you could spread passion dust on anyone anywhere in the world, who would you spread it on and what would you hope to accomplish?

Ford: I would probably say two things. And again this isn't a question that I would normally answer, so it's not like the questions I always get.

I would probably say that America's youth understand the potentially that they have available to them, not only through technology - I mean if you look at the YouTube stars right now, a lot of them are young. There's never been a time in history where you can reach as many people and create a platform. It has good and it has bad, as we've seen in the media.

So I would probably say America's youth, design your life. As far as what would you do with it? I would say make sure you're a steward of money. That's probably the biggest mistake I've made over the years. I've made millions of dollars. I've invented products.

Most entrepreneurs I know that have made that kind of money, they don't hang onto it, because they know they can make the money so quickly again. So rather than putting $10K a month away or whatever it is, I know that I can go do something and make that in a weekend.

I would say look at your finances and make sure that you really plan for the future more effectively. That's just my theme of the day. Start where you are with what you have and get rid of the excuses. Don't compare yourself to anybody else. It doesn't matter what success anybody else has had or didn't have. It's what are you going to do?

Caren: Great. Thank you so much. Just so much information. I know that our readers are going to want to reach out to you Ford.

I know you said you weren't going to give us any links, but I'm going to ask you right now, how do people reach out to you? What is your call to action? How can they reach you?

Ford: They can visit me at http://PrimeConcepts.com They can look at me at http://ProfitRichResults.com Those are probably the two biggest places. There are great videos at Prime Concepts. Or just go to YouTube and type my name in.

You'll find me and you'll find lots of resources and books. There's books on Amazon you can go to on different topics.

I would just say if you like what you've seen today, post something on Facebook. Post your comments, post your thoughts - good, bad, or indifferent. I don't care if you disagree. I'm not afraid to ruffle the feathers. This isn't a popularity contest where I want everybody to love me.

Yeah, I want people to like me, but if you don't, I'm okay with that too.

48

Caren: Well I want to thank you for being on the show today. So much value and so much content. And I know that our readers have a lot of choices as to how they spend their time. I want to thank you so much for spending your time with us today. And as always, we'll see you next time on the next episode of *The Passion Point*.

Goodbye everyone.

Honorée Corder

June 16, 2014

Caren: Hello everyone. Caren Glasser here. Welcome to this episode of *The Passion Point*.

The Passion Point is the show where we get to follow entrepreneurs and people that are following their passion and making a living doing what they love.

Today I'm really excited about our guest, Honorée Corder. She's a best-selling author of dozens of books. If you go to Amazon and just put her name in there, I mean you're going to see a whole list of things come up. I'm right in the middle of her newest book, *Vision to Reality: How Short-Term Massive Action Equals Long-Term Massive Results*, and it's awesome.

It's an amazing book, and it shows you how these STMAs, and she's going to talk a little bit about that, how these Short-Term Massive Actions can really take you to the next step.

She's a coach. She's a result-oriented coach and that's really important because a lot of coaches don't do that. They just talk and talk and talk. Honorée is not that kind of coach, so I'm really excited to bring her in.

I'm not going to talk any more about all the different stuff on her bio, because we're going to talk directly to her. So Honorée, come on in and say hello to our network.

Honorée: Hi everybody. I'm so glad to be here. I'm so excited.

Caren: I am so delighted. We just recently have met. This is really an honor for you to be on the show today.

So we always like to start the show with a definition of passion. And the *Webster's Dictionary* definition says that it's a *driving overmastering feeling or conviction*. That's what passion is according to *Webster's Dictionary*.

Honorée, how would you describe passion?

Honorée: I think it's the force within us that makes us do the thing that we must do, the thing we're on this planet to do.

Caren: I could ask you the next question and say, are you passionate? Do you have a passion?

Honorée: Yes.

Caren: How do you think passion actually plays out in individual's lives? How do you think it actually gets in there and helps you?

Honorée: Well I think what I was saying is it's the driving force. I don't always know why I do something. I just know that I am compelled to do something. It's the thing that compels me forward.

I know from working with people and watching people that they are compelled to do something beyond reason sometimes because if they don't, they feel like they're not living their purpose, they're not living

52

what they're designed to do, and they feel - how do you feel when you don't feel passionate?

Caren: Dead.

Honorée: Yes. Not good. So a lot of people don't listen to that knocking that says you need to take action. You need to do this thing. They end up just kind of giving up. You can see it on their face. You can see it in the way they walk and move.

But people who are filled with their passion and who are using that passion productively have a little something extra.

Caren: It propels them.

Honorée: Yes.

Caren: Now you have a very interesting name, Honorée. Where does that come from?

Honorée: It is Old French. My father took lots of years of French before I was born and when I was little. That was how I got my name, it means *cherished one* in French.

Caren: Oh, I didn't know that. I love that. Cherished one. That is such an endearment from your father, obviously, who showered that on you. That's beautiful.

So let's take you all the way back, or as far back as you'd like to go.

Honorée: Okay.

Caren: How did you get on this road of your passion and creating these multiple books that you've done, *The Single Mom* book series, *Single Dad* series? And then we'll get into the *Vision to Reality*.

Honorée: I have always had something in me that propelled me forward. Whether it was compassion or a desire to contribute, I think it boils down to when I figure something out, I want to help other people to figure it out without the pain that I went through.

I was a foster kid. I lived in a children's home. My first goal wasn't to be successful. It was to not feel like crap about myself.

I went in search of things that made me feel good. Some of the very first things I read were *Laughter: The Best Medicine* in *Reader's Digest*, because that's what would come to the house where I was living when I was a senior in high school. And I would read that and think, oh that's interesting. I would read stories of inspiration that were in *Reader's Digest*.

As I gathered self-confidence, I would see other people who weren't as far along on the path as I was. I'd feel compelled to turn around and bring someone with me and to share what I've learned with them so that they don't have to go through the same struggles.

Does that make sense?

Caren: That absolutely does make sense. So as you were taking this journey and as you walked this path, how did you end up with the *Single Mom* series and the *Single Dad* series?

Honorée: *The Successful Single Mom* was born as I was engaged and getting remarried. I had been divorced for about six years, and I was working at home, which I have for most of my adult life. I'm on the computer and I'm watching Oprah, and she's doing this makeover show.

You know how when Oprah had her show on regular TV, like ABC, NBC, CBS, they would do these makeover shows and they would bring out someone. But before they did, they always did the before. I think what they tell you when they're doing the before is they frizz up your hair. So they have this woman, she had half her hair in a scrunchie. She's a tiny little person, maybe 5'4", size 2. So they put her in a 2XL men's t-shirt, oversized sweats, and some slippers.

I think what they told her was look as pathetic and miserable as possible. Then we're going to take your picture. It's not just the before. It's the before as bad as it can possibly be. So they take the picture of her, and then they're bringing her out.

As they're bringing her out, they're doing the intro. This is Linda, she's 43 years old, and she's a single mom of two people. I remember this for as long as I live. Oprah said, *of course as a single mom, she's a schlimpa-dinkah. She's not taking care of herself. She's taking care of the kids and the house and her job.*

I don't think that Oprah meant that derogatorily. I think this is just how we kind of look at single moms. Well of course that's how she is. Of course she's going to have frizzy hair, half in and half out of a scrunchie. Of course she's going to wear clothes that were her ex-husband's that are 16 sizes too big. Of course she's not going to get a little spring in her step and putting a little eyeliner on. Of course that's not what she's going to do because she's a single mom and that's how we see single moms.

And I went, whoa! Hold the farm! Why do we view single moms as victims, not victors? Why do we view them as not the heroes that they are, the people that are being mom and dad and keeping the lights on and the kids in clothing and school and food and working and doing all the things that most single moms do? Why is it that they are looked upon the way they're looked upon? Very interesting.

So I'm engaged. I go into the bathroom. My now husband is in there. And I said, I think I need to write a book for single moms. He looked at me and he said, *you need to take your executive business coaching program, and you need to customize it for single moms. Then you need to find single moms and work with them so you make sure it works.*

Practical man - didn't want me to write a book about something that didn't work.

So I did. And that was the beginning. It was that passion of we can't have anyone look at single moms like that anymore. And by the way, I went through a very dark period as a single mom where that's how I felt. I felt how that woman looked.

Look as miserable as you possibly can. It's not that that's what was showing up for the public. But that's how I felt. *I've been married and divorced. I must be a loser.* What's possible was only so possible for me, because I have this handicap. I have this epic failure in my background. And I thought, *that is not true.* I had come through that and was making good money, had attracted a wonderful man into my life and was getting remarried. My daughter was doing great.

I knew all of those things weren't true. And I didn't want another single mom to feel that way. So I made the program for them. I found these women. I worked with them. That was an amazing experience. Then out of that, all of the other books have kind of followed.

Then you ask about *The Successful Single Dad.* Well I had a lot of single dads writing to me and emailing me and saying, *I love your book. Where's the book for dads?* And I'm like, *but I've never been a single dad.* And they said, *the book is applicable. Because it's not gender-specific. It's person-specific. What are the lessons that you need to learn? What are the gifts you need to take away from? What's your plan you're going to put together?*

They said, *I'm really just pretending everywhere it says mom that it says dad.*

Caren: That's fascinating. Because you obviously struck a nerve.

Honorée: Yes. And then I had a law firm say, *we have a lot of single moms that we work with, but we also work with single dads. So if you can get the Single Dad book, we'll buy some.* And I was like, *alright. Great. I'm in. Sold.*

So the *Single Dad* book was born. It's really interesting because in interviewing dads to put their stories in the book in place of the mom stories, what I determined is men are taking being parents much more seriously than they have in past generations.

Some of the men that I interviewed were very high-powered, very successful, wealthy men, who basically said to their companies, *I'm a single dad. And everything that I do is going to be customized to me spending time with my children and being home with them every night, because I have custody of them.* I thought that was very interesting, because we generally think it's the single moms, but then the dads go off and do whatever they want to do. I'm seeing that trend is less and less true.

Caren: I'm noticing that also out in the community, in the network and the people that I know, the men in particular. We're talking about men that are single dads that in fact if you go on Facebook, you watch, you literally see them with their kids. In fact, that's all they post about, because their families are so important.

What you're talking about is very interesting, because we tell people when they're trying to follow their passion and make a living with something they love is to find the pain point. Find something that people have pain about. And you just jumped right in.

You heard it on Oprah. I find that interesting all by itself, because Oprah's not a mom. So how would she know what a single mom feels like? But you found the pain point. You heard the pain point and you addressed it.

And then of course the men came and said, *what about us?* You heard their pain. And once again you addressed that. So you don't just talk the talk. You walk the walk. From that, tell us how your journey continued.

Honorée: Well this is a "three feet from gold" story. Because Oprah inspired the book, the women I was working on the book where I'm coaching them and writing the book, they were all convinced, as was I, that we were going to release the book, we were all going to send it to Oprah in little magical packages that were going to show up on her desk, and we would be on the show. Then we would help these millions of other single moms that - and you may have read this part in *Vision to Reality* where I talk about the thud that was heard around the world.

We sent the book off to Oprah and nothing, like crickets. It's that thing where I was like, *wait a minute. Hold on. I was told build it and they will come. I built it. And we've sold 12 copies. What is going on?*

What ended up happening over time, because I had put so much time and money into the book, time - writing the book, money - I hired a PR person who was highly recommended and had the price tag to go with it, and for whatever reason it did not catch on. I don't know if it just wasn't the right time or whatever. Maybe that was the universe saying, *hold on sister. We have something coming up for you.*

But nothing happened for a while. So I put it upon Amazon, and I got back to doing my executive coaching and my training. I thought, well maybe this wasn't the thing that was meant for me to help single moms. So we'll see. Over the next couple of years, however, every month Amazon would order more books.

Eventually my accountant said, *you may want to have your own bank account for this. You may want to have your own company for this. Because this is actually a real thing that you've got going on here.*

I went oh, alright. Then people started writing to me. I have a COO for my company and they're writing to her and they're saying, *you know, this program that you write about it in the book, where is it? Where is this program being held?*

This Single Mom Transformation Program, which was originally meant to - in the book I have a whole chapter that says, *listen, go get 10 other single moms and have a class with them and do the exercises in this book and be a community for each other.*

What we were hearing was we want someone to lead that. So I created the facilitator certification for the Single Mom and Single Dad Transformation Program. I have about a dozen of those around the US that hold these classes. So it's been this amazing journey where every time I think, *okay, that's it*. Something else happens.

I ended up writing the rest of the books in the series that I had originally penciled out and then thought, why would I write five or six books when one book wasn't doing anything? Now there are five books in that series. I'm just about to release the last, I think, book in the series in the not-too-distant future.

Caren: How did you make the leap then from the *Successful Single Mom* and *Successful Single Dad* to your newest book that's out, the one that I'm in love with. How did that come about? And let's talk about - so it's *Vision to Reality*. I want to talk about visioning, because that's something that we hear. We have to have that vision. So tell us how the book came about and why this has become such a movement?

Honorée: So the *Successful Single Mom* was actually my second book. My first book was *Tall Order*, which is *Seven Master Strategies to Organize Your Life and Double Your Success in Half the Time*. A mouthful.

I wasn't really writing books for single moms, Caren. I wasn't writing books for single dads. I was writing business and personal growth development books. I am a business coach. I'm a corporate trainer. I go in and train sales skills and business skills and growing your business.

So this single mom thing was really a tangent. It was an asterisk, like something that I was compelled by passion to do, but it was not the main thing that I was meaning to do. I kind of got off track - on track - whatever you want to call it and wrote those books.

In my mind *Tall Order* was the beginning of a series of books to help professionals, because then there's another segment of the world that

59

tends to, in some ways, be passionless and frustrated. And I wanted to inspire that.

Along the way, I created the 100 Day Coaching Program For Me, because I didn't like math. I wanted a program where I could have one day and it was equal to 1%. I'm just saying, let's make it easy, instead of a quarter that has 89 or 92 days in it, and you have to multiply and divide and all of that. Who has time for that? If I'm making my life happen, I don't have time for that.

So I created the Coaching Program For Me. Then eventually I realized that I was selling people on coaching by saying you're going to pay me a heck of lot of money and we're going to have a conversation. I realized I would not buy that. People were buying it, and I must be a great person. But where's the tangible?

I paid $400. I get an iPhone. It's madness. Quid pro quo. I pay you, I get something. So I thought, I have this program I use. Every 100 days I sit down and create new goals and new outcomes, the whys, and the whole thing. I wonder what my clients would think of that. So I rolled that out.

And all these years later, there are several different versions of that. I call it Short-Term Massive Action, so STMA. It's in the title. This book came about because not everyone can afford coaching off the bat. Not everyone knows about the fact that visioning (the verb), you have to go do some visioning to get the vision. How do you do that?

I wanted to be able to touch as many people as possible and help as many people as possible. It is much easier to buy an $8 ebook or a $15 paper book than it is to engage in a coaching program sometimes for some people. I wanted something for my clients that I could give them as a gift that would explain what they would be going through if they chose to coach with me or if they chose to coach with one of my coaches.

So here's an overview. Here's the psychology behind it. Are you ready? Let's go! Let's turn what is that you want for your life into the thing that you're living every single day. Then as we go, let's just keep expanding that and pressing the reset button every 100 days and see how far we can take this.

Caren: I was telling you before we got onto our interview today that as I was reading it, I was compelled to actually go into my calendar and block off a couple of hours to put down in writing my five and ten-year goals. As well as then you talk about bringing it back down to 100 days, 75 and so forth.

I know people are going to want to go out and buy this book. Can you give our readers a couple of things they can do right now without even getting the book, something they can do right now?

Honorée: Sit down and pull out your calendar and schedule two hours. Then start to capture in whatever way that works for you; writing in a journal, open a document on your phone, open Evernote, and create the *Vision for My Life* document in your journal, online, or however that works for you.

Just start to write down if time, money, space, love, everything was no object, anything and everything that you would need, where are you? Who are you with? What are you doing? How much money are you making? Where is the money coming from?

Where are you traveling? What are you driving? What are you eating? How do you look? And take away the limitations that exist today, if they exist. If you're not well, imagine yourself well. If you're not rich, imagine yourself as rich as you would like to be. And rich is not just money. Rich is love and space and time and having a clean towel when you get out of the shower.

Rich is anything and everything that you could think of. Capture that. Capture that vision and just start to make it more tangible than just the thing you think in your mind.

A lot of people think, I don't write down my goals. They're right here. And it's like, that's all fine and good, but it's important not to think it. You must also ink it. You must also get it down on paper.

Caren: Oh, I like it. Not just think it, but ink it.

Honorée: Yes.

Get it down so that then you can review it and look at it and create a mental movie about it. If they don't buy the book, if they don't do anything else, it's capture that vision and create that vision. Then twice a day close your eyes and visualize yourself riding in that convertible Mercedes on the Pacific Coast Highway with your hair in the wind (we would put it in a ponytail so it wouldn't get messy) with your favorite Starbucks drink in the cup holder.

And it's glistening and getting water all in your cup holder, and you're like, *it's just a Mercedes. I'll get another one.*

Who's in the passenger seat with you? You've got luggage in the trunk. What kind of luggage is it? Where are you going? What are you going to experience when you get there? Really live into that and take in the smell of the saltwater as it's coming off the ocean. What does it smell like? And what are you wearing? And how do you feel?

When you're at a traffic light, log into your bank account and see how much money is in there. Imagine your best client calling you and saying, *you have made my day. Thank you so much.* Really live into that.

If that's the only thing that you do, and you visualize that twice a day, they're going to wake up one day and go, oh, I'm driving down the Pacific Coast Highway checking my bank balance at the traffic light.

Caren: It's true. Are you familiar with Napoleon Hill *Think and Grow Rich?*

Honorée: Yeah. I think I've read that book 100 times. So, yes.

Caren: I read it every year. I read it every single year, because every single year I listen and hear something different in the book. One of the things I hear people say is, oh, we're just supposed to think it and it's just going to show up. Well, not necessarily. You're not going to just think it.

Honorée: No, but close. Not 100%, but that's on the right track. There is something very powerful about our minds I think we're just starting to figure it out. Visualization is that thinking part. I heard a great guy recently on YouTube, and I wish I could remember his name right now, but he was saying when you visualize, you visualize in the first person. It's you driving the car and drinking the Starbucks and having a conversation and checking your bank balance.

Then it's also you outside of the car looking down at yourself driving and drinking and talking. So the third person, and viewing yourself doing it, not just from the internal looking out but also the external watching yourself.

I thought that was very interesting, so I've incorporated that also.

Caren: I've actually, I've never heard of that piece before. I have a friend who talks about visualizing. And she actually takes the first person into account when she does her intention statements. Instead of just saying, *I am a successful business woman,* right after that she'll say, *my name is Caren Glasser.* Because the brain understands personal and can say, *oh that is true. That is your name. So maybe the other statements that you're making are true.*

How do you feel about that? Does that make sense?

Honorée: Oh absolutely. First, second, and third person. I'm doing it. I, Caren Glasser am doing it. You Caren Glasser are doing it. Caren Glasser is doing it.

Caren: Exactly. The unconscious mind versus the conscious mind. I think of it as like an iceberg. The tip of the iceberg is our conscious thoughts and below the surface are our unconscious thoughts. It's the unconscious thoughts that drive us, basically.

Honorée: That's right. That's very true.

Caren: So okay, we're going to talk about quotes. I love quotes. Quotes get me going in the beginning of the day, the middle of the day, and the end of the day. We're going to talk a little bit about our favorite quotes. I'm going to put out a quote today that I actually live my life by. And it's written by me, imagine that, I actually made my own quote.

Passion drives us, motivates us, and enables us to live the life of our dreams.

What is one of your favorite quotes?

Honorée: So something by Tony Robbins. *Anything is possible if you think it's possible.* And then I took that and said in *Vision to Reality,* "Committed eats impossible for lunch."

Caren: That's clever. I like that.

Now we're going to talk a little bit about things that I'm just always curious to hear. If you could spread passion dust anywhere around the world on anyone around the world, who would you spread it on, and what would you hope to accomplish?

Honorée: I would spread it on my daughter. What I would want to give her through that is, and what I'm really trying to do without the dust right now, is to give her the belief in herself that anything is possible that she wants to make happen. Whatever her passion is, I

64

mean, right now her passion is Justin Bieber and The Candy Jar, which is the little candy store that's in our shopping center.

Caren: She can do anything she wants.

Honorée: I want her to think she can do anything she sets her mind to, as long as it was for the good of everyone concerned.

Caren: That's wonderful. I think it's important we instill that in our children. I really appreciate the fact that you want to instill that in your daughter. I have spent a lot of time instilling that in my sons as well.

Mine's a little bit older than yours. He's now a young man. He's not a teenager any more, but I think it's so important that we instill that in our young people, because they are the future. They are who is going to be here long after we're not here anymore.

Honorée: Yes.

Caren: Absolutely.

Do you have a guilty passion?

Honorée: Yeah. I watch a lot of Bravo TV. I do.

Caren: Me too. It's fun.

Is there a song that you are passionate about? What song gets you going in the morning or in the afternoon?

Honorée: Right now my ringtone is *Happy* by Pharrell. I haven't gotten tired of it. I must hear it 20 times a day. And there's the 24 hours of happy, the website, where they just play the song over and over and over again. It never fails to make me happy, even if the person calling me doesn't make me happy. When my phone rings because I'm happy, I love that. So I'm passionate about that song right now.

Caren: If people want to get in touch with you and they want to maybe take the next step with you and learn how they can interact with you, where shall they go?

Honorée: http://CoachHonorée.com

Caren: Check it out, and also check out her books. If you are a single mom or a single dad, definitely go check out that series of books, the *Successful Single Mom* and *Successful Single Dad*. And of course, I recommend it highly, because I am right now in the middle of it, *Vision to Reality*. Go check that book out and get it.

I'm going to encourage you, even if you have an ebook reader, get it in a hard copy, because you're going to want to highlight, and you're going to want to make notes, and you're going to want to stop and go and do the program. I don't know about you Honorée, but even though I have a lot of books on Kindle, all my personal development books and my business growth books are in hard copy so I can make notes.

Honorée: Yes. I get them in all three. I get the digital book so I can always have it with me when I'm traveling on my iPad. I get it in paperback form or hard cover so I can make the notes. Then I get it in Audible so if all I'm able to do is listen to it.

Caren: I am just like you. Oh, it's good to know there are people out there that do exactly the same thing, because I thought I was crazy for doing that.

Honorée: You are crazy, in a good way.

Caren: I am, in a very good way. Is there anything that you'd like to share with our readers before we say good bye?

Honorée: Maybe someone reading is wondering if they can turn their vision into reality and they are not in a good place. We are clearly in good places today in our lives, and it shows with us.

But if someone reading is not in a great place, just keep putting one foot in front of the other. Put good stuff in. Read good stuff, watch good stuff, listen to good stuff, and eventually good stuff is going to come out. It has to.

Caren: Wise, wise words. Well, I just want to thank you Honorée for being on the show today. I'm so appreciative.

I want to thank all of our audience today, because you have a choice as to what you do with your time. And we are so honored that you chose to spend your time with us today.

So as always, have an awesome day. Go out and give someone else an awesome day. And we will see you next time on *The Passion Point*. Goodbye everyone.

Michael Krisa
August 21, 2014

Caren: Hello everyone. Caren Glasser here. Welcome to this episode of *The Passion Point*. This is the show where we interview Passionistas from around the world who are following their passion and making a living doing what they love.

Today, we have a very special guest, Michael Krisa from Ontario, Canada. He has a very unique style that demystifies video and video marketing. He makes and helps entrepreneurs have a much easier time with video.

He is the co-founder of Easy Web video, which is a great product for those of you who are getting into the whole video thing and want to make your videos look a lot prettier than they do when they're just on YouTube.

I know I'm a bad girl Michael, because I don't always do what I talk about. But we'll talk about that as well. Michael is also a licensed real estate broker, a syndicated columnist, he has podcasts, and is a freelance internet marketing consultant. He does just about everything. And more than that, he's just an all around great guy. So we're really happy to welcome Michael Krisa to *The Passion Point*. How are you doing today, Michael?

Michael: I've never been called a Passionista before. Do I need a blood transfusion?

Caren: It's a good thing to be a Passionista. It just means that you're passionate about what you're doing, and we have them all over the world, so welcome to the crowd.

We're going to start today basically by defining the word passion. *Webster's Dictionary* says that it's *an intense driving or overmastering feeling or conviction.* What do you think passion is, and how would you describe it?

Michael: There has to be that driving force for what makes you want to get out of bed in the morning, face the day, and do something. There are people that it's almost like a prison sentence. *Oh my God. I made it through another night. Now what do I do?* Versus the ones that don't want to go to sleep because they're burning that candle. They're wasting daylight and they want to go out and do something.

The thing that really stands out to me - and I wish I could say it's my quote, but it's not - it's actually Steve Martin's. Appropriately it came out New Year's Day. And it was, *be so good that you can't be ignored.*

To me, that's been my driving force for the past year. I'm passionate about what I do. But when I saw that - *be so good that you can't be ignored* - that just resonated. Everything I try to do now, I throw myself into it, and I want to be that guy that is so good that you can't be ignored.

Caren: I have never heard that quote before. I'm going to steal it from you. You already stole it, so it's okay.

70

I'm all about R&D - Rob and Duplicate. So that's a good one and a great definition of passion. You obviously are very passionate. You're a passionate guy. But you started in real estate. Before that, when you were a kid, you weren't doing real estate.

Tell us a little bit about your journey. How did you get from A to Z?

Michael: You're bringing back memories. I remember my parents cried bitterly as they packed me in a tiny little rocket ship from Krypton and blasted me out from my native planet.

Did you want me to go that far back or get somewhere sooner?

Caren: [*laughing*] You can do whatever you want. I'm just going to sit here now and have a good time.

Michael: I thought that's what editing is all about! But seriously, it's been a long, eclectic journey. Looking back, it's all these different skill sets that you never think would come together. It's like throwing fruits, vegetables, and meat into a blender. What the heck are you making? Soup!

That's kind of what happened. I got out of university and did the typical, *what do you want to do now?* I was a supply teacher. I was a bartender, bouncer, delivered mail, a scuba diver, all these different things. And every time I did something, it's almost like it opened up another door and another opportunity presented itself.

I've never shied away from going, *what's behind door number one? Let's go take a look.* And it's all these eclectic skill sets that have somehow overlapped that have given me a) the confidence to be in front of camera, because I teach people how to use video. So, go figure, that's important. Being able to articulate a message with passion, because I really sincerely believe in what I do. But more importantly, what I do helps other people.

Here's another one you can write down. I love this quote. People always ask, why do you share stuff? What are you going to get out of that? What's the ROI? And the thing that resonates with me is, *a candle loses nothing by sharing its flame.*

If you can share what you have, and it sparks other people, that's where real creativity comes, when you've got that blossom or that spark of an idea and people take that, run with it, and before you know it, you've got a flame that's changing the world.

That is my mission right now. Video helping small business. I know I'm rambling a bit, but man! When it comes to video, and what I've seen it do - even what we're doing right now, this is video. This is TV! You and I are doing live TV. How cool is that?

Caren: Exactly. It is so cool. If people only realized how easy this is to really get your message and who you are and your personality out into the community and create those relationships. I know you agree. This is your entire life.

Michael: It's all about creating that aura of know-like-trust. When people see you on TV, it can be something as small as their little iPhone. But our brains can't make the quantum jump from this is an iPhone, this is a computer screen, this is a kick-butt wide TV screen.

All our brains can conceive is it's moving pictures and sound. Since we're the purveyors of information on that medium, we become perceived as that authority, or what I call the celebrity authority in whatever niche we're trying to implement ourselves into.

Caren: It totally makes sense. And what do you tell people when they say, *I hate the way I look on video.* What do you tell them?

Michael: I say, *guess what! You're ugly. Get over it.*

What are you going to say? *You're beautiful.*

72

Deep down inside, yes, you are. In front of the camera, you're a pig, like me. *Get over it and have fun.*

Caren: Exactly.

Michael: Here's the thing. People will resonate with you, the authentic and in Caren's world, the passionate you. They don't want a cheap knock-off of what you think you should be. They want you to show up because they're looking for authenticity. If you can just be yourself, because everyone else is taken, man, you're already 90% ahead of the game.

Caren: Oh, I so agree with you. I just go and tell them, you look like you look. You look exactly how people see you. That is exactly how you look.

And exactly, get over it.

Michael: And that's what paper bags were made for. There's always that as an alternative.

Caren: You are absolutely hysterical. I want you to be on this show every single week because you're just going to completely crack me up.

Let's talk a little bit about failure, though, because a lot of people get caught up in *I don't want to fail. I'm on this journey, and I don't want to try something because if I fail, I'm going to feel bad about myself.*

I know that all of us who have been successful in what we do, we have failed a gazillion times. How about you Michael?

Michael: We've heard this before a million times. There was the invention of the light bulb. The story that you don't hear, the really cool back story of the light bulb, he already had the prototype done.

Let's pretend this is my light bulb. And when they were getting ready to test it, he gave it to one of his subordinates to carry the bulb. They're running through the lab, setting it up to do the test. The guy drops the bulb.

Drops the only prototype for the bulb.

So they have to go back to the drawing board and make another one, which took weeks, months, however. They've got bulb number two ready to test. Who does Edison give it to carry? He gives it back to that guy.

And they're looking at him, *old man with a beard, are you a fool? What are you thinking?* He says, *who do you think will take more care of that bulb than anyone in the room other than this guy?*

Caren: I have never heard that story. That is actually a much better story. I think that is powerful. Where do I find that?

Michael: It's called *Uncommon Friends* by James Newton. It's a story about Edison, Ford, and all the early thinkers. Newton interviewed all these great thought leaders and all their lives intersected. That was one of the stories about Edison. There are stories about Ford. It is just such a wealth of information about all the backstories of what was happening. How the tire came to change the world, what was happening when Ford was nearly bankrupt, all the stuff you never heard of.

So all these leaders - it's not like they woke up one day and said, *today I'm going to be successful and make a gazillion dollars.* No. They fall down. But I think the thing between a leader, an entrepreneur and a wannabe is an entrepreneur gets up and says, *I see what I did. What can I learn from this? And let's move forward.* Versus, *this guy is against me. I'm just going to sit here and wallow in self-pity.*

Caren: I totally agree. That's the whole Napoleon Hill, *Think and Grow Rich.* And that is a challenge for a lot of people because they think, *what do you mean? I'm going to think it and it's going to happen.* There's that missing piece in between. But he also did all those interviews with Ford and all the different individuals.

A friend of mine, Andrea Waltz, she wrote a book called *Go for No* with her husband Richard Fenton. Are you familiar with that book?

Michael: I'm going to say yes, but no - I've never heard of it before.

Caren: It talks exactly to what you're talking about it, and that is failing your way to success. I don't like the word failing either. However, it is just picking yourself up, dusting yourself off, keep going and moving forward and using your experiences to propel you forward. What do you think about that and using your experiences?

Michael: Let's get back to when you were born. You're a baby. If you didn't bang your head against the crib, if you didn't fall down and lose your suckler from time to time, you would still be in a crib.

It's from the learning experiences, bumping your head, getting dirty, making mistakes, but realizing they're not really mistakes. It's the forces that be are giving you a nudge in the direction that you should be going versus the direction you think you should be going. Maybe that's a better way to look at it.

Caren: Yeah, I think so. So what do you tell people that are looking for their passion, and they're looking for a way to create a new life for themselves. Maybe they've been laid off. I call them accidental entrepreneurs. They find themselves in a situation where they got laid off, fired, or downsized. And now they find themselves in a situation of, *I spent all my life at this nine to five job. Now I don't know what to do. I don't even know what I'm passionate about.*

What do you tell these people? Or do you even talk to these people?

Michael: It's not like I say, *you're one of those people. I see the signs. Don't come near me.*

I think I would probably start off with you've got 24 hours starting now. Wallow. Feel sorry for yourself. Eat Hershey's bars and peanut butter.

But 24 hours from now, you have to get your ass off the couch and decide what is it that you want to do with the rest of your life.

Who are the people in your life, the significant others, that are depending on you to be a success? I would look at that core first, and then reexamine what it is that really fires me up? We said this right at the beginning.

What is it that makes you want to get out of bed and say, *hot diggedy! I've got another 24 hours. What am I going to do today?*

I don't think there's a universal answer for what that is. That's a lot of soul-searching. But what is it that if you had to do it all over again, this is what you would want to do for the rest of your life.

There's that old expression, I'm going to paraphrase it: *if you do what you love, you'll never work another day in your life.*

Caren: Maybe you're still doing real estate, but how did you transition from real estate to Easy Web Video?

Michael: I lost a bet with God.

Caren: [*laughs*] And after that?

Michael: Well after he cashed in his chips, I made the transition from doing podcasting. I had one of the first podcasts in the real estate space. Then about four to five years into that, a buddy of mine, Mike Stewart, pulled me into this video thing kicking and screaming.

He said, *I'm doing a workshop in Atlanta. I want you to come down. Be my guest. You just have to get your hairy butt down here. We're going to teach you how to edit video.*

I thought, *cool. This is right on the cutting edge.* So my wife and I go down there. I've got my laptop. And there's 300 people in the room. And just to show you what the extreme was - on one side you've got people with a mouse thinking that it's something you have to give cheese to. On the other spectrum you've got guys that are literally with the CIA that are manipulating satellites in space.

And then you have us in the middle saying, *what to do? Edit. Okay. I think I got it.*

So I did what every typical entrepreneur probably does. Went home, took it, put it on the shelf, and then forgot about it, because there's that adage, *the only barrier between you and success is the cellophane around the last product you bought.* I do that on occasion. I buy the stuff with every great intention of using it, like the hair-restorer and all that stuff. I just don't get around to using it.

Caren: Oh, that's the reason.

Michael: Yeah, but my armpit hair: Huge. I just don't want to show that off here.

So we were on a trip to the Grand Canyon, and I was getting ready to launch my first digital product. And there's a difference between whether the Grand Canyon was in Canada versus the US. If it was in Canada, we'd have a fence. We'd have a plexiglass barrier. And there'd be a big computer monitor, and we'd be watching it, because they're all about safety and watching what we do.

In the US you actually have signs over the edge of the Grand Canyon that they want you to read, because I think that's a form of birth control in the US. Completely different mindset.

But the point is while we were there I was so inspired I said to Diane, *if we had that camera, I would be hamming it up right now.* She reaches into her backpack, and she pulls out this little Sony and says, *this one?* And from that point forward, a ham was born.

I was motivated by the surroundings. I had a message I wanted to share. Getting back to this whole archetype, it was all about the passion and having to get it out there.

Caren: I love that. That's a great story. And so you took that leap. Out came easy web video. So tell us, what does the product do? Because I alluded to it earlier that I was a bad girl.

Michael: Being on the Grand Canyon and taking a leap - I like that one.

I didn't take the leap. Let's just say I took small steps along the edge.

But how Easy Web Video came to be, Mike Stewart had a marketing event in Atlanta. I was there with about 300 other people. And I happened to be sitting at a table with a fellow Canuck. And once we started talking, he had one of the first online video players that would convert your video to Flash, which compresses video into a format that allows it to play on the web.

We started a dialog that we kept going for seven or eight years. I kept saying, *can we take your product and do this? What if we added that?* And the whole idea was I wanted it to do things I needed it to do and easy, because I'm not a tech guy. I told him, *it's complicated, I don't want to know. But if it's a matter of copying and pasting this, I'm in.*

And it just morphed from there until I became a partner. I bought into the company two years ago. And hence Easy Web Video was born.

Caren: It was revolutionary. It was basically one of the first of its kind. It allows people to take their videos and make them pretty.

Michael: So you shoot a video on your computer. Magically the fairies have to come lift that video off your computer and get it onto the internet for people to see.

I don't want to say we're the fairies. We're the pixy dust. We're the interface that will take the video, compress it into a format that will play quickly on the web, that will play on all these devices, because right now 60% of all traffic is on mobile. So it's key that people can access the information that you're sharing.

It puts it onto a hosted server and then adds effects like clickable images, lead capture forms, the ability to put your video into WordPress or onto YouTube. There's all these things that are built into the functionality of what we've done. But in a nutshell, it's taking the video off your computer and putting it up for the world to see.

Caren: It's very cool. And for those of you listening who are saying, *I want to see what this is all about,* here is the link - http://www.easywebvideo.com - go check it out. It's cool stuff.

Where do you see this whole video world going to? I know you just said you're not really a techie. But you are a techie. You are in the midst of where we are in the world right now of technology. Where do you see us going with all of this?

Michael: I'm holding my iPhone and I'm a PC guy. So for me to say anything nice about Apple hurts a lot, being a PC guy.

When I teach from stages, I'm a speaker. I'll be in front of 500. I'll hold up my iPad, but first I'll say, *show of hands, how many people here are using Mac.* And I'll see them and I'll say, *children, I want you to play amongst yourselves while I have a conversation with the adults.*

It's just a polite way of saying, look guys. It's never been easier to do video. Apple has made it easy, with the iPhone I can now shoot a video. I can edit it on my iPhone. I can upload it to the web.

So your question of where this is going, because the tools of production - and when I say tools of production, like an iPad, that is literally a $1M movie studio. In the day, you would have to have a whole filming crew, editing crew, all that stuff. I can now do it. Literally if I can finger paint, I can now be doing all this on my iPad or my iPhone.

So where this is going 1) the barrier of entry is gone. Anyone can be doing a video. But with that the barrier of what people will tolerate is now going up exponentially. Because the expectation is they don't want to see cat videos anymore. They're looking for something more

79

polished and professional. So you'll have to know how to do some basic editing.

Even though I'm making the faux pas here, you have to have some decent lighting, microphone for sound. People will forgive a shaky video, but if they can't hear it they'll disengage within the first five seconds.

There are these things that you'll need to know moving forward. Yes, I can do a video, but making one that people will actually want to watch, that barrier is going up. What I'm saying to the people that are watching us right now, you've got to get out there now, get your feet wet, fall down, make your mistakes like we were talking about, and start honing this skill.

Because where it's going, the estimation is by 2016 70% of all mobile traffic will be video. Which means 70% of the population will be walking in a stupor watching video. It has to be your video.

Caren: I 100% agree. And also the studies tell us that people will watch video up to 2.5 minutes in your website, and less than 10 seconds in static text. Now think about that for a minute. That's just crazy statistics.

You've only got one chance to mess it up. So if people come to your website, and you get them to your website, and there's nothing there but a bunch of words, they're gone and they're not coming back.

If you have stuff going on, and that means a video, or other things going on, that's why you need a person like Michael and his product. It makes it so much easier for people that do this.

So Michael, any last words you want to share? Actually, before we do that, I have a couple questions for you. I got so caught up in what we were talking about, I forgot the rest of my questions.

Michael: I have that effect on women, I know.

Caren: You do.

I love quotes. You've already given us a couple of quotes. I want to just insert myself here, because I want to share one of the quotes that I happen to like. And this one actually is anonymous. Nobody has taken credit for it, so I'll take credit for it. Why not? And that is, *purpose is the reason you journey, and passion is the fire that lights your way.*

I just love that. Any other quotes you want to share with us? Because you've already given us a few.

Michael: Another favorite is you look at something and it looks so complex. What can I do to get started? And it's the little things. There is one that is, *little hinges swing big doors.*

Caren: Nice.

Michael: Get started. By doing that one simple video, that will be the cascading effect that will get you to do the next, the next, the next. And as we say, you'll get better doing it. Small hinges swing big doors.

Caren: I love it. Like Nike says, *just do it.* Take that first step. It's scary, but once you're in there, the water is fine. Come on in and join us.

Do you have a song you're passionate about? What song gets you up in the morning?

Michael: Oh my gosh! I don't know. I'm a guitar-banjo-John Denver fan. I think when you ask, does anybody listen to John Denver? Everybody says no.

Caren: I do.

Michael: He sold 13 quatrillion albums. I guess I must have bought them all. But that's what got me playing guitar, banjo, and everything else. So maybe - I don't know if I had to have a favorite song, *Country Boy* is one that really fires me up.

Caren: I was about ready to sing. *Thank God I'm a country boy!* I love that song. That's great. So we have something in common there.

If you could spread passion dust anywhere around the world on anyone, who would you spread it on and what would you hope to accomplish?

Michael: I would think right now high school kids. Let's say school kids, generically. I'm not focusing on university, because they're already lost doing whatever they do.

Grade school kids have to understand that they are the future, not only in the US but around the world. And gone are the days of the *I punch the clock, I show up, I do my job, I go home, and when I retire 40-50 years from now, there will be a pension coming to me.* Those days are gone.

That was my parents' generation, my grandparents' generation. That's what they grew up in. There was no such thing as a secure job. Your future is basically unwritten. And I think that's the important thing. When you get put into the system and you learn the basics of whatever you learn in school, it's a system.

We've got to get these kids to expand their minds. And I hate that expression thinking outside the box. If you have to say that, you're already in a coffin. Forget the box.

They have to realize that it's a big, wonderful world out there. There are tools everywhere at their disposal. They have to reach out and start being self-reliant. It starts with doing videos, creating a web page, talking to people.

Stop doing this - walking around in this stupor, texting. Be able to look up at somebody in the eye and have a conversation. So if I was to sprinkle that passion dust, it would be look, everything is out there, no matter how bleak it looks, it is there for the taking if you're willing to stand up and do something about it.

82

Caren: Great, great message. My youngest son is 29 years old and I totally resonate with what you're saying. No job is a for sure that it's going to be there forever. He's had multiple jobs, because something will always happen. They'll close their shops. The retail store will go out of business.

He came to me a couple of months ago and said, *Mom, I want to be more like you. I want to be an entrepreneur. I want to not have to worry about my nine to five job. I want to do something that I can create for myself.* So I see that transition in our young adults just because of my own son, who are saying I don't want to be beholden to this nine to five because I know that any day it can just go away. And what a terrible way to live.

Our kids are living in a different environment these days. They are not going to have what we had growing up. They are going to have to work harder for it, or they are going to have to figure out a way to do it on their own and not depend on the nine to five. Would you agree?

Michael: Oh, absolutely. You mumble around saying, *I hate this a-hole that I work for.* When you're self-employed, you are the a-hole. You work for yourself. That's the benefit there.

We talked about the tools of production right now. It's there. Everything they could possibly need to start a business. It's not like in the old days when you had to rent the office and have a typewriter and a secretary. Everything you need is at your fingertips.

Caren: I sit in my home office in front of my computer all day long. Sometimes it gets lonely. But to your point, I like to take my online relationships offline. Even though my offline may actually be online.

Like we have an offline relationship, but it's on camera. And we now know each other, we've talked to each other, we have a communication. It's not like we're just a friend on social media. I always love that when people say, *oh, I'm friends with him on social media. I've never talked to them, but they're my friend.*

83

There's a commercial now, I don't know if it's running in Ontario, where these older individuals are sitting in a living room, and they say, *I want to show you what I have on my wall.* And they have on their wall pictures, they literally paste pictures, and they go *this is my wall.*

And then somebody that's sitting there says, *I don't like your wall.* And she says, *I'm going to unfriend you.* And she says, *that's not how it works.* And it's funny, because we now live in this world where everything is online and they forget you're supposed to take these relationships offline.

How many of your online relationships are you taking offline at this point and creating that real relationship?

Michael: Oh my gosh! I think the deep ones are like what you and I are doing right now on video. And thank you for wearing clothes this time. I really appreciate that.

Caren: [*laughs*]

Michael: But that's where the relationships come from. Once upon a time we would be doing this by fax. The machine would ring, I'd pull out a paper, and I'd be reading this ink about your latest thought or what you're doing.

And this medium now, video, it feels - and I use that word purposely - *feels* like we have a relationship, like we've met. And getting back to what I do when I teach people about video, the astonishing thing is when people do meet you physically, they feel like they know you, even though they've never met.

So you and I have a friendship developing here because we're making contact and we're in a dialogue. But when people are watching your videos and they haven't met you, they've already made that decision in their mind that you're either a knucklehead or they're somebody that they can know-like-trust. That's important. I can't remember the term for that. It will come to me in a minute. But in their brain, they make this connection that you are now their friend, which is powerful. They've made the decision.

Now when they meet you in the street and say, *hey, Caren, how are you doing? Did you get any more penguins lately?* And you're suddenly going, *who is this person? Do I owe them money? Have they been following me down the street?* And then the light bulb comes on, *oh. They're watching my videos.*

Caren: How exciting is that though? I mean, for those of you listening out there, the technology is there for the taking. We're using technology that right now in terms of this video is available online. It's absolutely free, at least at this point. I don't know where Google is going to go with all of this. You can do this too. And you can connect with Michael later to make those videos sing and have bling and be out there.

So Michael, now I'm going to ask you the question. Are there any last thoughts that you would like to share with our listeners and our viewers before we say goodbye with them?

Michael: Last thought means I'm being put on an iceberg somewhere. I'll still be here. I hope we do this again.

I would say a departing thing would be you have everything it takes. Not to get metaphysical or whatever. But if you look at a seed, like a little acorn, you look at the acorn and you look at this big, beautiful gnarly tree that's 200 feet tall, the tree didn't know what it was doing, but it was all contained in that acorn.

I would wager that everybody watching this right now is like that acorn. They have everything it takes to be that 200 foot tree. But the first thing they need to do is plant themselves, because that's what a tree does. It takes roots. Get focused on what you do, what you want to do. And just get out there and start doing it.

Caren: Great message to our readers. Thank you so much Michael for being on with us today on *The Passion Point*. We really do get so much information and so much knowledge and so much emotion from the individuals that are on the show. So I want to thank you for taking time out of your day.

And I want to thank all our readers, because we know you have a choice as to what you do with your time. And we are so appreciative that you chose to spend it with us. So make sure today that you go out and give someone an awesome day. And we'll see next time on the next episode of *The Passion Point*.

Have a great day everyone. Bye bye.

DINA PROCTOR
APRIL 30, 2014

Caren: Hello everyone. Caren Glasser here. Welcome to this week's episode of *The Passion Point*. This is the show where we interview Passionistas from around the world, finding out what their passion is, and finding out how they're making a living doing what they love.

Wouldn't you like to do that as well?

Today we have a special guest. Her name is Dina Proctor. She is a coach, a business coach and a life coach. And she's created this very, very cool thing, for lack of a better word. It's called Meditation 3x3. She's going to talk about that.

She's also the best-selling author of *Madly Chasing Peace: How I Went from Hell to Happy in Nine Minutes a Day*. I am sure our listeners want to know how you did that, and I would like to welcome you Dina to the show.

Dina: Thank you so much Caren. It's such a gift to connect with you. And I'm honored and excited to be with you. Thank you for inviting me.

Caren: The pleasure is all mine. We like to start our shows with a definition of passion, according to *Webster's Dictionary*. It's kind of dry. It's kind of boring, but we'll let you tell us your take on passion as well. *Webster's Dictionary* says that *it's an intense driving or overmastering feeling or conviction.* That's what passion is according to *Webster's*.

What says you, Dina?

Dina: Oh, I love that. When I feel passion, that's when I feel like I could do something all day long. It's something that I love immersing myself in. It re-defines my entire being.

It's me connecting to that which is greater than myself. I always say I'm on the 3x3 bus, but I'm not driving it. So that feeling of just relaxing into that greater wisdom and having that free-flowing feeling, that passionate feeling flow through me, and knowing that as I connect into that deeper awareness, I am uplifting and inspiring the lives of others.

For me, that's passion.

Caren: And I'm watching you talk, and I'm listening to you talk, and it is obvious the passion is just bubbling out from you. So I would venture to say I wouldn't even have to listen to the words that you were saying. I would know you were talking about passion.

You're awesome!

Dina: I love it! Thank you.

Caren: Let's talk about your journey. Let's talk about how you got to the 3x3 Meditation and your take on that journey. You can take us all the way back to when you were a little girl, if you like, and come on forward into the present. So tell us your story.

Dina: Okay, yeah, I'll start where it gets kind of interesting. It was about five years ago. That's where I hit my rock bottom in my life. It was the end of 2008, and even as a little kid I was a real perfectionist. I couldn't have an A- grade. I needed an A.

I always had to do everything perfectly. I would make little schedules for myself. At 7:02 I would wake up. At 7:03 I would brush my teeth. At 7:12 I would do this - my morning routine. I always had this real perfectionist thing.

I don't know where that came from. No one else in my family is like that. I can't point to my parents instilling that in me. It was just something that I accept as part of who I was and how I was forging my identity.

That perfectionist tendency I think is a lot of the root of what ended up taking me down to where I hit my rock bottom five years ago when I was 32 years old. When I was in my 20's, I struggled with depression. I was diagnosed with major depressive disorder in my early 20's. I was put on medications, and I went to one-on-one therapy and I went to group therapy. And then I was put on anti-anxiety medications.

I felt like there was this hole inside of myself, this void. I think that's what the perfectionism was doing. I had this inner restlessness inside of myself. I needed something, a way to control myself or control my environment in order to make me feel safe and secure and okay.

So in my 20's, that manifested itself as I was having this deep, deep disconnection and this major depressive disorder. In my trying to fill this void, I found myself very restless in the areas of my life. I was changing jobs every nine months. It was like, *I don't feel happy here. I don't feel fulfilled here. I need to do something else.*

I was volunteer of the year. I have presidential awards from all the volunteer work I've done. I've worked with homeless people and in shelters. I've been to Africa and Guatemala and done fundraisers and worked for non-profits, because I felt like if I can just give enough of myself that will fix me.

Caren: Oh my gosh! I am listening to you and I am saying, *I resonate with that!* Keep going!

Dina: It's funny because - I'll get back to the story, I promise - the work I do now in helping other people, it's fulfilling in a way that the other work I'm doing never was. And it's not because I wasn't doing good work. I was doing great work. I was helping people with their lives. But that wasn't what I was put here to do. That wasn't my passion, my life purpose.

Now that I'm in tune with my life purpose, there's nothing more joyful than being able to uplift and inspire other people through my method and my message. That was my thinking. But I wasn't going about it the right way.

I was changing jobs, upgrading my boyfriends, moving to new cities. And *oh, I need roommates. That will fix it.*

   -Wait, I want to live alone. That will fix it.

   -I need to be single. That will fix it.

   -Wait, I need a boyfriend. That will fix it.

That was just how I was. Towards the end of my 20's, I found alcohol. And it's funny, because I was never a huge drinker, even in college. It just never really appealed to me. I didn't like the feel of alcohol being in my body.

But towards the end of my 20's, I had spent 8-10 years trying to solve this problem and trying to fix myself, and I was at a new point of desperation where alcohol really could just enter and take hold. And take hold it did!

That became a huge, huge addiction for me. I just went down fast with it. I was partying six nights a week, and just drinking around the clock. I needed a drink to get out of bed. I needed a drink during my lunch break at work. I needed a drink, obviously, at nighttime.

When I started drinking so much I began doing things that I didn't like myself for. I was becoming a morally not-such-a-great person. I started stealing money. I was lying to everyone. I was drunk at work. I was using people, especially men. And I couldn't live with who I was becoming.

I sure couldn't quit drinking, because that was the only thing that was making me feel better. So it was this place of *I just wished I was dead.* I wished I wouldn't wake up in the morning.

I had that wish for years. On and off throughout my 20's and my depression, it was like *gosh! If life is going to be this hard, I don't even want a part of it. I can't figure it out. Just take me out of here.*

But when I started becoming that morally - I guess decrepit - individual, I couldn't live with myself anymore, and that's when I chose a date to take my own life.

I unintentionally ended up in an addiction recovery plan. That's a whole other story altogether that we won't go into right now. But in the addiction recovery program, when I finally surrendered to it and agreed to go through the steps and the process of it, the woman that I chose to mentor me instructed me to learn to meditate.

And I remember looking at her like, *yeah, meditate? Shouldn't that be like beating on pillows? Or venting out my feelings? Or writing letters?* It just seemed completely impractical to just sit still. What was that going to do for me.

But she was very tough love. And she said, *if your way had been working, we wouldn't be having this conversation right now. Why don't you try my way for a while?* What was I going to say? No?

Caren: Exactly.

Dina: She was very good for me.

So her instruction to me was to sit still for 20 minutes every morning and focus on my breathing. And I thought, how hard can that be? I don't think it's going to do anything. But I'll do it. And the first few mornings, Caren, when I tried to sit still for those 20 minutes, I would max out at about the three-minute mark. It was just physically impossible, because I was in withdrawals. I still had all these negative suicidal thoughts.

It was just physically impossible for me to sit still for longer than three minutes.

But she had told me 20, so a couple hours later it would nag at me. You know, *I only did three minutes. Maybe I should sit and do a couple more now.* A couple hours later, *I would think, maybe I could do a couple more minutes now.* So that by the end of the day I could tell her that I did my 20 minutes.

Caren: You were a perfectionist and you wanted to follow the rules.

Dina: I had to follow the rules. That was exactly right. That was her one instruction. I was a perfectionist. I was going to do it!

So that's what I did. And I would call her at the end of the day and tell her, *I got my 20 minutes done. It's messy, but I did it.*

She was supportive of me through that. *Whatever you can do, Dina. Whatever you can do, keep doing it.*

What was amazingly fantastic, like the huge gift that came out of this messy three-minute here, three-minute there thing was about eight weeks after that process I found myself in a state of no mind chatter. I never even knew that was possible.

I was completely at peace. I can only describe it as a state of higher consciousness. My awareness was physically above and behind my body. So I was hovering, it was like there was there big ME essence that was hovering above and behind my body for three whole days.

I had no mind chatter. I was in this deeply peaceful, blissful state but also fully present in everything I was doing. And when I was interacting with people, all I could see was their soul essence. All I could see was the essence of love energy in their being, whether or not they were connected with it. That's all I could see. Anything else just faded from my vision.

From that experience, I mean, once you know that and once you've been in that state, you can't not know that anymore. I learned a couple of things while I was in that state.

The first thing that was obvious to me was that there is no such thing as time. It was really like cute that we all run around - *oh I'm late. I'm overwhelmed.* To me, in that grander state, it was just very obvious that there was no such thing as time. There was no need to be as urgent as most people were.

Also it was very obvious to me that anything I wanted to create in the physical world, whether it was a healing in my body, an improvement in my relationship, better financial situation, everything was created from this big essence energy first and then reflected in the physical world. I had been busy doing it backwards my whole life. I was changing jobs, changing boyfriends, getting new cars, manipulating my exterior world thinking that would fix the inside.

It's backwards. So finally I saw that. No one told me, but I had the experience that if I get the inside right that's all I need to do and the outside then follows.

From there is where 3x3 got created. It means three minutes, three times a day of this focused meditation time period. And it's not just sitting still and focusing on breathing. It's an active visualization of what you want to create for yourself.

Caren: So how can someone start a 3x3 Meditation?

Dina: If you want to start a practice, say that you have a goal. And I've been working with individuals the past couple of years. I'm starting to work with businesses too, which is really exciting.

Most of the clients that come to me are either having a problem in a relationship or having a problem with the body. They want to lose weight and they've been stuck. They want to manifest a better career.

Everybody who comes has a goal and has just felt stuck for a while. They have this back of the mind knowing or a belief that if they could just get their insides right, their thinking right, that this will happen. So those are the people that I work best with. Those are the clients I tend to attract.

When I coach people through a process, I tell everyone take it seven days at a time. Say that you want to lose 50 pounds. I've heard from various different experts that it takes 21 or 28 days to change a habit. So I'm not saying that in seven days the habit will change. But I am saying that if you play full out with the new mindset and new behavior technique for seven days, you'll feel differently than you did seven days previous.

Then from that point, seven more days, seven more days. And after three to four weeks, you can say, *my gosh! I really do think differently about this than I did three to four weeks ago.* So I always encourage people to take it in those smaller increments. Because the key is not how many times can you do it over a span of three to four weeks. How many 3x3s can you do, or how many meditations?

The key is playing full out with it, being able to hold an intention, a new belief, or a rewired brain pattern in place constantly and consistently over short bursts of time. And enough short bursts of time strung together create that new neural pathway in our brain. And then we start thinking differently about it.

I could talk about how to start a weight loss - we could go into detail about how to do it, but I always encourage people, seven days at a time.

94

After seven days, take your temperature. How do you feel? Renew it. Refresh it. Go onto something else.

Caren: That makes so much sense. I mean, truly. It's just chunking it down to smaller timeframes. I like that.

Can you lead us right now in a meditation so we can get a sense of what that is?

Dina: Oh yeah! Let's do it. Okay, great. So we'll just do something simple. And this can be something that people can use for stress relief or just to re-center themselves during the day if they feel thrown off a bit or whatever.

So Caren, if you want to participate, or anybody watching if you want to participate, my eyes will go open and closed. You can choose which one is most comfortable for you. If you like to keep eyes open or eyes closed.

I encourage you if you've been sitting, I've been sitting in this same position. So I might shake out my body a little bit. Kind of renew my presence in this space right now. Even if you have limited mobility, you can even just move your head or shift a finger, just to renew your presence in this space right now.

Just let your body become still and become quiet. Let the chair that you're sitting in hold you up completely. No need to exert any effort right now. Just let your physical body come to a place of stillness and relaxation. As you feel your body relax and your muscles, any tension just completely releasing, you may also notice that your thoughts are relaxing. It just feels good to let your mind settle in and have some space there for a minute.

As you become still and present, bring your attention gently on your breath in this moment. No need to change the way that your body is breathing, but just become aware of it, aware of this small miracle that breathing is. As you become focused on your breath, imagine that you're breathing in the essence of what you would most like to be feeling right now.

For example, it might be a sense of peace. Or it may be a sense of accomplishment. Or it may even be just a little bit of relief. Find the essence of what you most wish you were experiencing right now. As you breathe in every inhale, you're taking in that essence, and it's trickling down and infiltrating and saturating every cell of your body.

Every time you inhale, just imagine that peaceful or joyful essence is gently entering your body, and it's able to travel up through your mind, through your head, and all the way down through your body, just touching and infiltrating every cell.

Just stay with your breath, a couple more breaths, just like that. Breathing in that peace, that healing, that presence, infiltrating every cell of your body.

And just let yourself take one last breath, just like that. A last full breath [*inhale*]. That essence trickling down, every cell of your body, every fiber and dimension of your being, just feeling it completely infiltrating you right now.

Then you can release that visualization and that intention. When you're ready, open your eyes or return your attention to the room.

Caren: I can see how this could be very soothing if people make this a part of what they do. I feel myself completely just go *whoosh*.

Dina: Yes, and it doesn't take that long. It's about touching in that space. You're not doing it just once a day to check it off the to-do list. *Okay, I went to the gym. I had breakfast. I had my shower. I meditated.*

No.

This is a space to live from. It's a mindset. It's a place to live from. It's a state of mind. It's a state of being. And that's why for me it's really important, it's more important for me to take smaller increments throughout the day than just one longer one and check it off the list.

Caren: So why is mindset so important? You've mentioned the word mindset, and I talk about mindset as well. But why is mindset so important in order to achieve results?

Dina: This is a really great question. The point of mindset is because a lot of us, let me use weight loss or health just as an example so we can tie this down, make it tangible.

For example, if I know that I want to lose weight, what do I need to do? I need to eat better and exercise more. So that's just kind of common wisdom. If I take the approach of, *I'm going to use my willpower. I know that I can just discipline myself. I'm going to eat this amount of calories a day, this much carbs, this - I'm going to itemize it all down, and then I'm going to run every single day and go to the gym and lift my weights. And I'm going to use willpower and discipline to get this done.*

Well if we've been out of shape for a while and have not been in this, it's kind of like an awakening, a little bit of a shift for our body to get adjusted to. If we continue to use just this willpower, without changing our mind about it, without worrying about our mindset, without focusing our mindset, we're just focusing on our physical results and powering our way through it, we're going to reach a time when we max out.

That's when we start to feel deprived. *I should eat these carrot sticks, but I really just want to eat a cake.* So we're feeling that deprivation like, *I don't want to go running. Please don't make me go running today. I really should. I'm going to muster the energy. I'm going to go running.*

All of this is a good jumpstart. It's in our lives for a reason. If we're in an emergency situation or we're starting something new, if it takes a few days of transition to get the mindset under control. Willpower can serve us, because it will keep the engine going. It will keep the behaviors in place before the mindset comes in.

But that's not a sustainable, long-term solution. That's why so many people, I think, fall off diets. I'll give you an example about deprived eating. I have this intuitive eating practice that I developed. I know a lot of people do intuitive eating. I didn't know that when I created it; I thought it was all brand new.

I have this practice that when I go out to eat on my intuitive eating practice, I look at the menu or in the pantry or what's in the refrigerator and just ask my body, what are the cells in my body calling for? Keeping my focus soft, taking in everything, not really attuned to anything, and just seeing what lights up for me, what pops for me, what feels appealing for me, and honoring that.

This is a very simplified version of how I do it, but when I eat like that it's a very satisfying experience for my body, and I have no feeling of deprivation, because I have honored what the cells were calling for. I gave them what they needed. And there's no sense of deprivation.

Now, when I was first developing this practice, I was invited to go out to dinner to this Italian place. And I love this Italian place. I always get the lasagna, like this huge helping of lasagna, and that's what I was craving. So they invited me for dinner. It was 9 a.m., and immediately, my mouth was watering. *I can't wait for dinner. I can't wait to get that lasagna. I'm so excited.* I had that craving.

So I went out to dinner. It's 6 p.m. I pick up the menu, and I was like, *I don't even need to look at the menu. I know what I'm getting.* And I remember, *wait a minute. This is not how I eat anymore. Let me do my intuitive eating.* I just let the thought of the craving move to the side for a second, and I looked at the menu, and I said, *okay body, what looks good to you?* And there was this vegetable wrap thing and I thought, *you know what would be really good? All those veggies.*

There was zucchini and cauliflower. I don't remember what. And I just thought, *that would be so good sautéed in some garlic and olive oil.* So I asked the waitress, *can I get that?* And she said, *I don't see why not. Sure.*

98

And the thoughts of the cravings of lasagna just left me, it didn't nag at me like I was feeling deprived.

The meal came, and I ate. It was so satisfying. I was mindful like I was eating. I was fully present. I was with people. This isn't a practice where you have to be alone. Everyone's looking at the menu. I'm just doing something different as I look at the menu. It doesn't take any extra time.

And then as I'm eating, I'm being mindful about it. I'm just noticing that this beautiful food is nourishing my body. My body knows how to extract exactly what it needs and discard anything it doesn't need. And I had this really satisfying dinner.

Now if I would have gone to the same restaurant without my mindset having been changed, without the intuitive eating in place, I would have gone to the restaurant and thought, *I really want the lasagna but I shouldn't. I really just should eat the vegetables. Ugh. Alright. Can I just get the vegetables?* And had a resentment about it, or this sense of deprivation about it.

If I would have gone home after that not-so-satisfying meal, I may have been setting myself up for a binge either that night or later on. So do you see the distinction?

Caren: That's fascinating, actually. I had never really thought of it in that way. So that's a nugget that I'm taking away from our interview today. That's actually very fascinating.

What do you tell people that are lost. They've lost their passion. They've lost their mojo. They can't seem to get back up on the horse. What do you tell people?

Dina: It's such a good question, because sometimes - well I haven't felt like that in a long time, but I used to. When I was depressed it was just, there's nothing here for me. Everything here just seems like it's such hard work. I have no idea what I really want to be doing. How can I even find that out?

Well I believe, because I'm living a dream I didn't know that I had. If you would have told me I was going to write a book and share my story with the world three to four years ago, I would not have believed you. I didn't even want that. That wasn't even something that was on my radar that I wanted.

I'm telling people that so that even if there's something that is not even on your radar as a possibility, that doesn't mean it's not a possibility if certain things about your life shift. Just stay open-minded, stay really intuitive and adopt a curiosity about it.

It's the same way like Caren, if you and I were sitting on the side of the road, and I said, *Caren, watch and count all the red cards that go by.* So we sit for five minutes and you're counting them, and I say, *how many white cars did you see?* You would be like, *I was counting the red ones. I don't know if there were any white ones going by.*

The point that I'm making there is that we see what we focus on. It doesn't mean there weren't any white cars, but we weren't focused on it, so we didn't notice them. So the point that I'm making is that if we're looking at it as, *there's no passion for me. I don't know where I'm ever going to find my passion. There's nothing here for me.* We're not creating the space where we could possibly see it.

We need to just soften about that a little bit and become kind of curious about everyone else around me, a lot of people are finding their passion. I believe that there's something for everyone. I wonder if there could be something for me. I'm willing to keep my eyes open. I'm willing to be able to see.

More important than any of that, I'm willing that if something intuitively comes to me - a class to take, or a coffee shop to visit that I don't normally - and I'm just feeling intuitively drawn to meet different people or go up to someone I normally wouldn't have, I'm going to honor that. Because that may lead me down a path I wouldn't have otherwise experienced.

You know, I was inspired intuitively to take a writing class. I had no idea that was going to eventually lead to a book. I quit the class. Six months later I hadn't even touched my writing. It was like, *I'm done.* But then different synchronicities of people I met held that vision for me.

Even if you're involved in something and can't see where it could possibly lead, that doesn't mean that there's not a bigger plan or a bigger path. It's about cultivating that openness and that curiosity about what's possible.

Caren: I like that word, that curiosity. I think that's something we can all latch on to.

So I'm all about quotes. I don't know about you, but I'm all about quotes. I like to talk about my favorite quotes. I'm going to ask you to share one of yours as well.

Today's quote for me comes from a gentleman named Jay Silver. He writes, *my idea of a perfect world really can't be designed by one person or even a million experts. It's going to be seven billions pairs of hands each following their own passions.*

Dina: Ooh, I like that.

I don't know if I could top that. That's a good one.

Caren: I have a feeling you can.

Dina: Well I'll share my favorite quote. I actually put this in the very beginning of my book, because it's a quote that really spoke to me. It's Deepak Chopra. And he says, *chaos is only an illusion. If you're seeing chaos, you cannot see far enough.* I'm butchering it a little bit. But it's like, *if what you see is chaos, you're not seeing far enough.*

I just thought that's such an amazing quote, because knowing if I'm too close to something I can't see that bigger picture, like if you're too close to a painting, you're not going to be able to see what the bigger picture is, what the artist was really going for.

Stepping back and being able to see, like I see how the laws of the universe, the laws of attraction are all working. My mindset is working to create my reality here. So if what I'm seeing looks chaotic to me, it just means I need to step back and get a bigger perspective. I'm not seeing from far enough back.

Caren: Great, great advice. And so taking that one step further, take a step back, if you could spread passion dust anywhere around the world, on anyone around the world, where would you spread it and what would you hope to accomplish?

Dina: I think what I would do - I love the passion dust, if I could sprinkle that everywhere. My big dream is of course, 3x3 Meditation changed and transformed my life. So my dream is to see it available to anybody in the world that it resonates with, to be able to be uplifted by that.

But even bigger than that, I would love to just hold the message out that meditation, mindset, visualization, all these interior work techniques, that every single person has access to them, whether we know it or not. Just opening that door so that they're able to realize, *wait a minute. I have access to power I may not even know I have. And there could be a technique or a process or a person or an inspirational book to awaken me to that, to be open to that.*

So I think that's what I would want to be universally available around the world.

Caren: And there's no question Dina that you're going to do that. You're driven, obviously. You're motivated. I'm not going to call you a perfectionist, because you're not. Right?

Dina: Nope!

Caren: I am sure that you're going to meet your intentions, your mindset is certainly there. So one last question before we start to close off our interview here. And that is do you have a guilty passion?

Dina: I left guilt behind a while ago, because it wasn't serving me. But I get what you're getting at, something -

Caren: Chocolate.

Dina: Yeah, I know. I do like chocolate. I enjoy eating. I enjoy food. I like trying different foods and things. So I might go with that. I like watching movies and stuff too.

Not to the point where it's unhealthy - because I used to have an addiction mentality towards stuff. And what makes it different now is I don't necessarily need it. I enjoy it, but if it was taken away from me, I would be okay with that.

Caren: Well, Dina, it has been absolutely a pleasure talking with you, and I'm sure that our readers are wanting to know how to get in touch with you. So let's give them something to hold onto. Your website is www.dinaproctor.com but is that the only way? How do they reach out to you and get in touch with you?

Dina: Oh yeah. I try to keep my website so that everything about what I'm doing and my work is on there. That's the very best way to find me. It's MadlyChasingPeace.com. There's a contact and audio meditations, information on the book, I've got a video series. I just like to have all kinds of different resources.

I have YouTube videos. They're free. A newsletter, and I try to pack that with some good video content every couple of weeks as well, but that is the absolute best place to find out what I'm up to and get in touch.

Caren: I know that you have a subscription, because I'm subscribed to it. I get a daily 3x3 that just gives me a thought for the day or something to do, and it's awesome. So for those of you who are listening, get on over to the website and sign up, because you can get a little piece of Dina every single day.

So Dina, again, thank you so much for being with us today. And I want to thank all of our readers today. We know that you have a choice as to how to spend your day. We are so blessed that you chose to spend it with us today.

Have a great afternoon everyone. And we will see you next week for the next episode of *The Passion Point*. Goodbye everyone.

KYLE WILSON
JULY 10, 2014

Caren: Hello everyone. Caren Glasser here. Welcome to this episode of *The Passion Point*. This is the show where we interview Passionistas from around the world who are following their passion and making a living doing what they love.

Today, I'm so pleased to introduce our guest. His name is Kyle Wilson. He is the founder of Jim Rohn International, that's where he worked for 18 years with his mentor, his collaborator and his business partner, Jim Rohn. We're going to talk a little bit about that as we get into the interview, because anyone who is in this field knows who Jim Rohn is. I'm just so excited that we have Kyle with us today.

During that same time, he created, produced, and published over 100 personal development books: DVDs, CDs, programs. You name it, he's done it. Every time Kyle and I talk, I'm just blown away by what he has done.

He's also the author of *52 Lessons I Learned from Jim Rohn and Other Great Legends I Promoted*. He's a co-author of *Chicken Soup for the Entrepreneur's Soul* with Mark Victor Hansen and Jack Canfield. I'm sure you've heard of *Chicken Soup for the Soul*. He recently launched Lessons From Network. This is his most recent endeavor. I'm excited to be a part of that as well. This is a community that connects people and brings mentors and trains professionals.

This is awesome Kyle. Welcome to the show. Come on in and say hello.

Kyle: Caren, thank you so much. That's awesome. Thank you.

Caren: I read your bio and I read this stuff about you. As I said, we've been talking for several weeks now. Anyone who has followed you and has seen what you've done at what point says, *really? You've done all of that. How can that possibly be?*

I know that you have. I've seen the products. I've seen the inventory and I've seen what you've done. You have done it.

So we're going to talk about how you did all this and you came to where you are today. But first let's talk about the word passion. *Webster's Dictionary* says that it's an *intense, driving or overmastering feeling or conviction.* That's what *Webster's* says passion is. What do you say?

Kyle: Wow! That's powerful. Passion is something heart and soul, that's one of my favorite mantras. Something you can be heart and soul in. I think we've all experienced being on both sides of that equation. I'm always looking for something I can dive into fully.

I know after 18 years, I sold all my companies. I had a couple of years where I played Mr. Mom and I was retired and trying to be balanced. And really my life became very unbalanced. Passion is when you're totally sold and totally into something.

And that's a gift, right? Being able to have something that you can totally give yourself to. But that's where the staff of life is. It's not about holding on. It's not about how much stuff you can get and create. It's really about experiencing things with other people. I mean, you find passionate people and they're committed to a project. Nothing's more powerful.

Just to give you an example, look at sports. You'll see a football team, a high school, college, pro team give their lives and pay a price that you don't see in the workplace, because they're playing for something. They're playing for the ring, the championship. And the camaraderie that comes from that is unbelievable.

Looking at that is something that I tried to create with my companies, with my team, and it's a way of life.

Caren: So let's talk a little bit about your story and how you have come from A to - I'm not going to say Z because I know you have a long journey ahead of you. So let's talk a little bit about Jim Rohn and how did that all come to be. Talk about that time of your life. I know you have some stories.

Kyle: Totally by accident. I grew up in a tiny little town. My first business was a detail shop. I worked myself up over five years to having the biggest service station in town. Ten employees. We were open 24-7. Wilson's Texaco, *we're America's station.* And I was an entrepreneur and went through all kinds of experiences by the age of 23.

I decided to move to Dallas. I started the detail shop here and there's no reason in the world I would have ever met Jim Rohn let alone partnered with him. It was two years later I went to a seminar and the guy putting on the seminar was looking for salespeople. A couple of years later, I was his top guy, and we started promoting Jim Rohn on a small level in little towns.

I went off on my own and started doing big events. I would have a couple of speakers. I would have Og Mandino or Jim Rohn or Brian Tracy. And a couple of years later after that, 1993, Jim was independent.

107

His partnership had not worked out. I made him an offer he couldn't refuse and the rest was history.

So it's nothing you could have set a goal to accomplish. It's nothing you could have prayed. It's nothing you could have designed. It's just one of those things incredible opportunities that just happened that I will forever, besides being honored and blessed by it, I feel an obligation the rest of my life to fulfill a calling to have 18 years with that man.

Caren: Absolutely. And I would venture to say that it changed your life.

Kyle: Of course. It was his philosophy. I had started reading some success books. I had read Tom Hopkins, I read the *Magic of Thinking Big*. I don't think I had read *Think and Grow Rich* until after I heard Jim.

But Jim Rohn, Caren, literally I produced hundreds of products and done all these different things with all the speakers, and edited every single thing we've ever done of Jim's, and I would still put on Jim Rohn in the car. Jim's the go-to guy for me. His philosophy - every time I have an 'aha!' that I want to take credit for, no, Jim said it first. I'll see where the root of it came from something Jim had taught me or shared.

Caren: I know from the people I have interviewed and the people I have crossed in my network, to a person, every single person knows who Jim Rohn is. He had an impact in my life. He's had an impact in so many people's lives. I can only imagine what it must have been like to work so personally with him.

I can't even imagine actually.

Kyle: It was a very unique relationship, because one thing with Jim, he actually - it was funny - he did not want to be famous. He would say *fortune over fame*. I remember getting a three-book deal with him with the biggest person out there, the biggest book agent, Jan Miller. Tony Robbins and Steve Kubby's agent. We had it with Simon and Schuster. It was huge. And he turned it down.

There's a whole story behind that. But we had an interesting push-pull relationship, because I'm such a marketer-promoter, and he was such a philosopher. He was very humble. So many speakers are big because they're good marketers too. Jim was a pure philosopher, the real deal. So it was a great marriage.

But like any marriage, I had to always have the foot on the brake a little bit, and I'm pulling him along more than his comfort zone. I'm so thankful he trusted me. It took a while to build that up. I'm so thankful he trusted me to let me push the envelope a little bit. I have some funny stories about that.

Caren: You want to tell us one of those stories? I'd love to hear one.

Kyle: One that just comes to mind as I'm saying that. It was 2001, and I'm doing a three-day event. We had Zig Zigler, Jeffrey Gitomer, Bob Burg, and Charlie "Tremendous" Jones. So it was Jim's two-day, these other speakers, and all kinds of cool stuff.

I had the film crew. We had the room set up, the big stage. And so Jim's just getting on stage. He's got his white board. I've got all this stuff going on ahead of time, and music playing. And then the lights go out, on purpose, and we're starting to play Van Halen, *Right Here, Right Now.*

I'm just sitting here with goose bumps, the excitement, the electricity, everyone's so excited. And he gives me this look, *this is kind of silly. Do we really need to do this?* Because he was so humble. He just wanted to go up on stage, do this, *what did the cow say to the farmer on the winter's day?*

So things like that. I look back and say, *that's awesome. That's funny.*

Caren: I would venture to say that was exactly what made him the top in his field. His humility. So let's fast forward a little bit. After you sold the company, which you were with him for 18 years, you said you became Mr. Mom for a while. You traveled your path. Now you have

109

launched Lessons From Network. Tell us a little bit about that and how it's going to help so many people.

Kyle: Yes, thank you. The evolution of it was we had launched Your Success Store, DenisWaitly.com and ChrisWidener.com while I was also doing Jim Rohn. I had this whole portfolio of speakers and products and things that we were doing and it all really cross-pollinated. It was magical to have that combination of exposure. So everyone benefited.

There was a high school football team that I was really passionate about, they had won the national championship. I just saw all these cool things. So I bought the domain LessonsFromSports.com and I interviewed the coach. It was just one of those write in your journal, something I want to do. That was 2007.

I sold the company. It was a whole series of events I never planned on doing but it was a team decision. We had 20 employees and with my top leaders, we all said this is going to be the right thing for all my speakers and everything we were doing. And I started thinking about this Lessons From Sports.

One day I started checking on these other domains and there's Lessons From Selling, Lessons from Social Media, Lessons from Accounting, Lessons from Baseball, Speakers, Authors, everything. So I had about a thousand "Lessons From" domains. I also had non-compete that I was having to wait out, and I was very disciplined about waiting it out.

I just thought I always preferred promoting Jim and Brian versus trying to do my own book or trying to go out and speak. I had spoken a little bit in promoting Jim. But I knew I was a true promoter, marketer. And I so appreciated other people's talent. I was always fascinated by anybody's talent, no matter what it was. You could be a photographer, and I'm sitting there trying to help you better market your business.

So *Lessons From* is a community connecting talent with the marketplace. We've created a platform where it doesn't matter if you're a professional in real estate, insurance, a speaker, an author. We want to create a membership site that provides all this content to help you do all the things we were really good at that most speakers were not good at. Things like building a list. I've built a million lists through all our publications. Things like creating content, creating products to sell.

Most talentedpeople have struggles on the marketing side. So we've created that platform. Additionally, we have the community aspect, being able to network with one another. We have some pretty big names that are a part of this, so the associations you get with the Jeffrey Gitomer or Chris Widener or Bob Burg, a Ron White, some of our different *Lessons From* experts, allows people, whatever profession you're in, to be part of that coolness of saying, *hey, I'm connected with Jim's 18-year partner, and Jeffrey Gitomer's part of it. Some of these other people are part of it.*

Yet we have that common theme of helping each other and connecting and networking. We do it through social media and events around the country. Then we have monthly calls and all kinds of ways that we connect the dots to make that happen.

Caren: I know people are probably wondering right now, who is this for? If I'm a business owner, is this something I should do? If I'm a housewife, is this something I should do? Not to disparage - I'm a housewife. But if I work at home, meaning I'm a parent, would this be something for me?

So who is this for? Is this for basically anyone?

Kyle: That's a great question. I'll tell you who my avatar has been. I think it's going to continue to grow. But initially the avatar I had was the people who would come to our Jim Rohn events. And the people that really stuck around and wanted to be part of the inner circle and connect. You would find it's a doctor, it's a high school coach, it's a fireman, it's an attorney, and of course it was speakers and authors as well.

Most of them that really went that extra mile, stuck around, wanted to get connected, down deep inside they'd say, *I want to do what Jim does. I want to share my gift, what I've learned the last 20 years. I want to share it with the marketplace. I want to speak, write a book, coach, and make a difference in people's lives.*

I've had thousands of submissions come to me, thousands. It has been from people from every walk of life. So literally I do think it's for everyone that wants to learn. Our membership site provides them, with all the content they need for growing their business. How to list build, how to create opt-ins, how to do all those things to build their business. They are also big Jim Rohn fans, and love being in that environment.

To me it's a very philosophical principle based approach to success. It's community-based. So typically I'll find they're Jim Rohn fans. We have that in common. And yeah, they want to grow their business. They want to grow what they're doing. Thirdly they want the associations. They want the networking with like-minded people.

Caren: Well it's obvious you're passionate about this. There's no question. So the next question I would really like to ask and brainstorm with you is that I have people come to me all the time and say, *I don't even know what my passion is at this point. I don't know how to find my passion. I don't know how to follow it.*

What do you tell people who have lost their passion? How do you help them?

Kyle: Everyone has fallen off the cliff before. Everyone has hit a wall. Sometimes you have to go out and try different things. That's one thing. I know people in their 40s-50s-60s that will find something that finally connects with them. And I think first you have to go back to being a seeker.

Some people are like, *it's never happened to me.* Where do you begin? You have to start seeking. If you don't have a passion, start seeking, asking. That's part of it - however you feel about prayer or meditation or whatever it is, but seeking. If you seek, you'll find.

As you're seeking, it's amazing the people you meet. I have to admit, I was seeking. That doesn't mean I deserved to meet Jim Rohn. Of course it doesn't, but I was seeking. It's not like I wasn't totally ambitious to find something to give myself to. So that's number one, you've got to be seeking.

Then you've got to put yourself in the right position. I'm a big believer in personal development, listening to tapes, reading books, getting around other people. We really are influenced by all the people we're around.

Look at your environment. I'm not a big believer in cutting people off. I see a lot of that on Facebook. *I'm going to cut people off. They're my problem.* You're probably equally the problem. But there is something to be said for getting around other influences that can help give you a different perspective.

So I think it begins with seeking and searching it out. It's amazing, I'll use the word serendipitous, it's amazing the serendipitous relationships we'll stumble upon. And sometimes we might hit three or four walls before that happens. That's where the not giving up, not giving in to the fear, the doubt, the worry, the despair. But staying positive, and having faith. I don't know of anyone that reaches any kind of success where they didn't have to exercise that muscle of faith to say there is something for me.

And that's what makes it special, right Caren?

Caren: Absolutely.

Kyle: When you've had difficulties and challenges and obstacles. I think all of us that have had incredible things happen, we could cry if we really told the deep story, because there was so much triumph over challenges.

113

Caren: Right. And I'm sure you would agree Kyle that for a lot of people if they don't even know where they want to be or if they're not seeking, which is a great word. I love that word. How are they going to know when that opportunity shows up in front of them? If they're not already in that process and in that journey of manifesting those intentions, so to speak. How are they going to know if it shows up in front of them?

Do you have books that you recommend to people. I know I have books that I live and die for. I tell people, this is my top 10 list. What are some of the books on your list?

Kyle: Well you've got me very curious. You've got to tell me some of your books real quick, if you don't mind.

Caren: *Think and Grow Rich* is number one. Number two is *The Slight Edge*, which is an amazing book. I'm drawing a complete blank on the gentleman who wrote it.

Kyle: One of my best friends, Jeff Olsen. I got the Jim Rohn testimonial for him on that.

Caren: Oh, well there you go.

Kyle: It was in real time when he was writing that book that we were collaborating on him and Jim doing an interview together for it. So anyway, go ahead. I'm sorry.

Caren: So we have similar tastes. That's an awesome book. And now I'm even more impressed with you. Then another, *Eat That Frog*. Being able to chunk things down to small sizes. And then again, along the same lines, also with *The Slight Edge*, chunking things down to small pieces so that you don't look at the big project or the full goal, the full intention, and say *there's just no way I'm going to get from A to Z, because I have no idea what those steps are in between.*

So those are some of the books that I like. What's on your list?

114

Kyle: *Think and Grow Rich* is at the top. My 18-year old son was asking me, *Dad, if I could only read one book* - he's about to go off to college. And he's done some personal development. I remember giving him a journal, and we've gone to some events, and he would fill out the journal and he would actually type up the notes and send it to our whole Jim Rohn list of notes. So some cool things. But just kind of with a clean slate, he was saying, *what would you recommend?*

We started going through the list of books, like three days ago and I think it depends on where someone is. *Think and Grow Rich* is a phenomenal book, but I think you have to already be there a little bit, because it's not an easy read. It's in the head.

For me, Og Mandino's *The Greatest Miracle* and *The Return of the Rag Picker* was a phenomenal book. *The Greatest Salesman in the World* by Og Mandino. *The Magic of Thinking Big*. I remember reading that book and that was powerful. *Acres to Diamonds*.

Caren: There are so many. And I remember a post you put on Facebook earlier about *The Four Agreements*, Don Miguel Ruiz

Kyle: Oh yeah.

Caren: Oh my gosh. Is that just one of the most amazing books ever?

Kyle: Absolutely. A good friend of mine is Robin Sharma. I like Robin's books, *The Monk Who Sold His Ferrari*. Darren Hardy's a really good friend, and he did a book similar to *The Slight Edge* called *The Compound Effect*.

Of course, they pay homage to Jim Rohn, because Jim Rohn was the daily disciplines. Both those books will tell you that it's Jim Rohn's philosophy. They came from the - you don't eat nine apples in one day. You eat an apple a day. It's the compound effect.

Caren: Exactly. What do you think about Stephen Covey?

115

Kyle: Love Covey. Earlier when you mentioned Jim being such a powerful speaker because he was the real deal. He wasn't a promoter per se, I would always compare him and Covey. I would say Covey was the corporate - his message I felt in particular was more corporate-oriented. And Jim's was more entrepreneurial, but they had that similar purity about just being a speaker.

Not saying that would make anyone else wrong. And Denis Waitly is the same way. Denis Waitly is just this pure speaker, content guy who's not really put a lot of marketing into it. And I love seeing speakers who market. I believe in that. So there's not a right or a wrong. But that is something that's very powerful about Covey and Jim Rohn, Denis Waitly, Og Mandino. It's just this pure message.

Caren: So the message to our listeners is that basically we could talk for hours about the books and the authors that we have read and read over and over again. I literally read *Think and Grow Rich* once a year. At the beginning of the year, I open the book and read it again.

I used to give out a copy of that book to anyone that came onto my team. But you're right, you have to be in a particular place to even understand it. It's in some spots it is very intense, actually.

I'm all about quotes. I know you and I actually had a conversation about this, and that will be for a whole other interview. But quotes are my things. I have a quote that I'm going to share today. I'm going to ask you to share a quote with all of our readers as well.

Today's quote, I don't even know who wrote it. It was anonymous, and that's literally what it said, but I love it. It said, *purpose is the reason you journey; passion is the fire that lights your way.* I just love that quote. So what's a favorite quote that you'd like to share with our listeners today?

Kyle: Off the top of my head, Jim Rohn's *learn to be happy with what you have while you pursue all that you want.* I think that's phenomenal advice. I did a lot of quote books for Jim and Zig and Brian Tracy and different people before Google. Before the internet.

You could turn to any page and the wisdom of all the different quotes, there's so much great stuff out there. I did on Facebook a couple of days ago, one from the movie *Bruce Almighty*. I love to get quotes from movies, like *Groundhog's Day* is loaded. So yeah, you can find such great stuff everywhere.

Caren: I agree. For me, I just like starting my day with something that's inspirational, and then in the middle of the day, I've been known to put quotes on Facebook that are not necessarily profound, but they're funny. If you really look at them, you can see the meaning behind them. And you want to touch people where they are, don't you agree?

Kyle: Yes. Also I like Jim's *don't wish it was easier. Wish you were better.*

Caren: I like that a lot.

Kyle: It's a very long quote where he has that whole series of *don't wish for less problems. Wish for more wisdom.* He just takes you through this whole different series. But that every day, *don't wish it easier. Wish I was better.* This is an opportunity to grow.

Don't be frustrated. Be fascinated.

Caren: I like that. It's very helpful.

Kyle: You're stuck in traffic or you have a weird conversation with someone or something happens or AT&T cuts off your phone and they're not supposed to and instead of being frustrated, be fascinated. Turn frustration into fascination. I mean, that's very helpful.

Caren: I like that. I used to use the expression *I'm just so crazy busy I can't do anything.* And someone actually suggested I change my mindset and say, *I'm fully engaged.* And I love that. Now when I'm crazy busy and I'm all over the place, I say, *I'm fully engaged right now.* It has a very soothing way to frame me instead of feeling crazy, I now feel that I'm very involved and engaged.

So I have a question to ask you, and it's a silly question, but you'll understand what comes behind it. That is, if you could spread passion dust anywhere around the world on anyone around the world, who would you spread it on and what would you hope to accomplish?

Kyle: You know, obviously your inner circle, right? I've always been - and I am involved in things outside of our country, on two different continents. Very involved in philanthropic things I'm passionate about. But I also think everything begins with inner circle - your family, your loved ones, the people close to you.

That's where I would spread it first, because it's that nucleus where things really happen. The ripple effect really happens. So I would say that.

Caren: I like that. I'm sure people right now are reading and saying, I have to get in touch with Kyle. I have to get to know him better. I want to find out more about Lessons From Network. How do people contact you?

Kyle: Sure. I have http://KyleWilson.com and I do have a free e-book called *52 Lessons I Learned from Jim Rohn and Other Legends*. And it's got 52 lessons of real-life stories from Jim, Og Mandino, Brian Tracy, Mark Victor Hansen, Les Brown, Harvey McKay and more. It's really a powerful book. And you can go to KyleWilson.com and get that.

I also have links to Facebook, LinkedIn, and Twitter accounts as well as links to the Lessons From Network page. In fact, you'll find that a lot on my KyleWilson.com page.

But http://LessonsFromNetwork.com is the main portal of everything we do. We have experts on all kinds of topics. You can click through links and find out all about them. It will take you to that specific Lessons From page. If you want to become part of it, there's details on that page on how you can learn more about the network.

Caren: Awesome! Well I know that our readers are going to go there and clicking their little hearts away, because there's just so much information. I only hope they don't get on overload and say there's just too much. You do have a lot of stuff going on!

So Kyle, any last words you'd like to share with the listeners before we sign off here?

Kyle: You know, Caren, I've really enjoyed this. There are several things you were saying that we could have talked for 30 minutes to an hour. I wanted to know more. I loved what you were just saying about you're crazy busy versus fully engaged. I'm going to adopt that. Thank you, that's now mine too.

I love collaborating with like-minded people. That's where the energy is. That's where the life is. So that's what I would say. It is so cool when things come together and you meet people that you have synergy with. I think if I had to give one last piece of advice it's something I did with Jim Rohn. It's what I did with all the other speakers. And I've watched people that have done it with me and who haven't.

It's always try and bring as much value as you can. When you bring value to influential people, they do take note. I think that's a great piece of advice for everyone. Find out how you can serve, like Jim Rohn says. Find out how you can help. That's how you really get on the receiving side, to come in and say what can I give? What can I bring?

I know that's the way you've been. That's how Kim Somers-Egelsee has been. That's how so many of the people that I have long-term relationships with. Either I've been the ones approaching it that way, or they were, or we both were and I think that's the starting point.

Caren: Powerful, and I agree with you 100%. How can we support first? How can we give first? Because people do business with people that they know, like, and trust. Create that relationship first.

I am just so thrilled that you took the time today to be with us Kyle. You just have so much information. We're going to have to do another interview, because there's just so much more that I would like to learn from you and I know that our readers would as well.

And readers, we know that you have a choice as to where you spend your time. I am just so honored that you chose to spend your time with us today. So as we do each and every week, go and give somebody an awesome today. We will see you next time on the next episode of *The Passion Point*. Goodbye everyone.

NANCY FERARRI
SEPTEMBER 17, 2014

Caren: Hello everyone. Caren Glasser here and welcome to this episode of *The Passion Point*. This is the show where we interview passionistas from around the world who are following their passion and making a living doing what they love.

Today is no exception. We have the amazing Nancy Ferrari here with us today. She's the host of her own radio show, aptly called *The Nancy Ferrari Show,* on W4CY radio, which she has been hosting for over four years. She focuses on sharing what's right in the world, and features guest experts who are making a difference.

Nancy is a passionate speaker, author, and contributing writer for numerous online publications. She shares her message of inspiration and living an empowered life. She's also the co-author of several books including the soon-to-be released *Loving with No Boundaries.*

She's passionate about being a member of the board on The Little Light Project, and she shares her expertise with sensitive and intuitive children. I just love what you do, Nancy and I just would like to welcome you into *The Passion Point*. How are you today?

Nancy: I'm fantastic and it is such a pleasure to be here with you. I'm also excited to be on your webcast as I speak often about the power of connection and this is a great way to connect! Now people will see how animated I am when I host my radio show as I use my hands a lot when I talk!

For those who don't know me, one of my passions as an intuitive visionary is that I facilitate vision board sessions, and I am passionate about creating my own. As I share my vision board with you, a manifestation is occurring as it says, *lights, camera, action.* Here we are sharing the lights, camera and ready for action!

Once again, thank you for having me on your show. I've been wanting to do this for a long time as this is my first webcast interview.

Caren: I'm happy we are your first, then! This is very, very cool. You've done radio for a very long time, so this is just another dimension. I think it's great that people are going to see you live, because I talk with my hands too, if you've noticed.

Actually I normally walk and talk with my hands. I always have to make a point of sitting in my chair and not moving.

Nancy: It's part of our expression, as I'm talking with my hands right now too.

Caren: Absolutely. So today we're going to be talking about passion, about what it is, how you manifest it, how you find it, and more specifically how did Nancy Ferrari find her passion and how did her journey take her to where she is today.

We like to start our show with the definition of passion. And who better to get a definition from than *Webster's Dictionary*? So *Webster's*

Dictionary says that *passion is an intense driving or overmastering feeling or conviction.*

That's what *Webster's* says. What does Nancy say? What's passion to you?

Nancy: There's one word that came to mind, which is *feeling,* because passion is what lies within us all. As I was just interviewed earlier today about this topic, I shared that I allow myself to go back to when I was born to access my true calling and passion.

In our reality, I acknowledge that we aren't able to access memories of our birth. However, what I know is that I have energetically taken myself to that place to discover the passion within my voice. I learned to share messages of inspiration, share them with others, so they too can experience living in their true calling, being so passionate that when they wake up to welcome the world to whatever is going to show up.

Every day for me is that place now.

Caren: I love that.

Nancy: It's such a great feeling to live in this space and do what I love. We've all had that particular job that paid the bills much as I did during the years of raising our three children. But that was not a passion and I made the best of it. There are positives as I draw upon 20 years of legal experience within my own business now.

However, what I'm doing now is something I'm very, very passionate about.

Caren: Well, you know, it's funny you say that. We've heard that expression, do you work to live, or do you live to work? What's your answer?

Nancy: I don't even call this work. I really don't. I am living in my true purpose and my true passion and it's all an immersion and integration of being linear and creative.

Caren: You've been doing this for quite a while. Let's go back into Nancy's life. Let's take you - maybe not all the way back when you were just born. But let's talk about this whole journey that you started on, where did you start? How did you end up with a radio show and touching so many women?

I know, we've had the opportunity now to meet and chat. And I know a little bit about your journey. Let's share a little bit with our readers, how did you get to here from where you were on this part of your journey?

Nancy: It's part of my work as a "life transition expert" within our association in Lessons from Network. It was after I made the conscious decision after our youngest child went off to college; *this job is no longer serving me. I know there's more out there.*

For all the people that are asking themselves, *now what?* Who actually now go, *who am I? What am I really here to do?* I started seeking and searching and discovered that direct sales wasn't in alignment with what I was seeking for.

There's always a gift in everything. This is what I'm very, very intentional on sharing. My career as a radio show host actually started from my social media posts about the benefits of drinking alkaline water and how to be more healthy. It was from those posts that someone asked me to be on a radio show. This was four years ago in April.

It just really wasn't what I envisioned how the experience would be which prompted me to take a leap of faith. I said, *I could do this.* It made me realize that I had not expanded on my college major of journalism and communication, and the fact that my kids said, *Mom, you could make a tree talk; do what makes you happy.*

124

I remind them of that when they comment on how busy I am now. I remind them that they were the ones who inspired me! I had my learning curve of navigating through BlogTalk Radio, and in time, the show started to flow, and guests were coming my way through referrals and publicists.

It was within my first interview in 2011, I was inspired to become a Certified Vision Board Coach based on my conversation with the author of *The Vision Board: The Secret to an Extraordinary Life*, that opened my eyes to what's possible. Six months after creating my vision board, I was offered an opportunity to host my show live in a studio, which I had manifested in my very first vision board. At the time of my creation, I was hosting my show on BlogTalk Radio and just used my phone for the interviews. It was amazing that I placed an image of a microphone and words in red neon light "Live On Air." What I knew for sure was that I had set the intention for the in-studio opportunity. Never knowing how, nor when it was going to show up.

That was a great experience because you feel the energy being in-studio. But a year later, it just wasn't the right fit, and right before I said I'm moving on, this opportunity within this network showed up. So it's been just this amazing ascension of one step at a time and not putting too much force into it and developing relationships with not only radio show guests that I've had, but their publicists who really get me and what it is that I want to share as an energy broadcaster.

I refer to myself as a conduit for my guests to share their message

Caren: So what is this show that you're doing now, the one that you've been doing now for four years on iHeartRadio? What exactly is the idea of the show? What kind of guests come on? And why would someone want to listen to you, other than that you are totally fascinating, and I love listening to you?

What are people looking for when they find you?

Nancy: When you were asking me earlier, clarity is such an important element that comes with your passion. When you're clear on what it is that you aspire to create... it took me a couple of months to identify what my show theme was about. I wanted to have a show that would allow my guests to feel comfortable to share what they do and inspire my listening audience.

It's all about inspiring the listeners that there is an abundance of infinite possibilities waiting for them. A big message in my show is to encouraging others to dream big in life. When we think small, that's how the world appears. There is so much out there to experience. When you can share that with someone who's feeling like there just isn't anything out there, it is my intention that whoever I have on my show is sharing their transformation and what they're doing inspires others.

I've interviewed some acclaimed authors who have a closet full of books that no one would even read and now all of a sudden they're NY Times best sellers. Someone once told me I should interview celebrities. I asked, *why?* Just because they're well known, well, they're already well known. There are a plethora of people out there who are here to share their story and how we can relate to it. So it's all about how together we share what's real, relevant and relatable.

Caren: I love what you're saying Nancy, because really at the end of the day, you're approachable. Your guests are approachable. I understand when people say, *why don't you interview celebrities?* Well celebrities are not us. We don't really relate to that other than maybe there's a desire to be rich or doing something that a celebrity is doing.

But more in terms of just the people that are actually making a difference, and we can actually connect and make a real distinction as to, *I really relate to what that person is saying.* I'm sure you get that kind of thing when you get real people on that are sharing their stories, right?

Nancy: Exactly. And for me, when I listen to a show, if there's a takeaway, then I know that there is value. I want to provide value to people, because we don't often get to connect or hear the voice behind someone who has either created an amazing coaching program or is an author or is well versed within what they do with health and wellness.

That's why I love live shows. That's why this is fascinating for me to be seeing you in that I feel really almost a more sense of an immersion with you. That's my goal is to take this to possibly a stage. Someone once gave me a divine compliment that I remind them of Oprah in the sense that I just create a very comfortable place for them.

Once you're comfortable, then that's when the real and authentic you comes forth.

Caren: Absolutely. That's when the magic happens. I think when people feel comfortable and their authenticity comes out, they feel like, okay, I can be vulnerable. And I don't know about you, that's been one of the hardest things that I have had to tackle as an individual, being vulnerable.

Because I tend to - you're on radio. I'm on internet television. I do some podcasts as well. People tend to think that people like us are different. And we're not. We're just like everybody else. The reality is unless you start being vulnerable with your community, that's when they don't think that you're like everybody else. How do you feel about being vulnerable?

Nancy: Just like what you said. I mean, my generation was, *children should be seen and not heard.* Well, I had a message, I came into the world with a big message. My mom even said I was literally laughing at two months old.

Well I must have been drawing on something from another life to be doing that. But yeah, now that I went back in time, I wanted to answer your question.

Caren: Vulnerable.

Nancy: Being vulnerable, yes. That wasn't in. You don't brag about yourself. You don't share your dirty laundry. This and that.

When I feel it's appropriate, and there again, someone made an assumption, which I am all about *The Four Agreements*. That *Nancy, you possibly couldn't know what it's like to struggle.*

I'm like, really? Just because I came here well-groomed because you go to a studio, you want to look your best. You feel more confident and all that. But I'm still me. I'm still me in here. Give me the opportunity to share that with you.

Now what I'm going to share with you is that I do know what it's like to be in a space of - how shall I say this? - because my parents were born in Finland, I had that WWII mentality surrounding me of scarcity. We value everything. We don't even throw away plastic bags and this and that.

I feel that I am very relatable in that if someone's talking about someone losing a job or possibly having to leave the country due to circumstances, I've been in that space. I can say I understand.

Caren: You've been doing this show for four years. Recently you got involved with a non-profit organization called The Little Light Project. Can you tell us a little bit about this and why it touches your heart so much? What you're doing with them, and maybe how others might want to get involved?

Nancy: I would love to. I had the privilege of being introduced to Kirsten Hathcock from a mutual friend, Shelly Ehler, who was also on Shark Tank. Kiersten is not only the founder of The Little Light Project, she is also the President of ModMom Furniture. It was my intention to interview both women and set the wheels in motion to seek them out.

128

I'm giving away some of my trade secrets. If you want something bad enough in life, you ask for it. Shelly could have said no, but she wanted to be on my show, and then she said, *Nancy, the more I'm getting to know you, I really want you to meet Kirsten. I think she'd be great for your show. But I also sense* - and there we talk about activating your senses. *I sense that you should connect with Kirsten about The Little Light Project.*

I said yes. So we met, and I will never forget, I was out in the backyard. That's just where I feel more in my element with talking with someone. And when she started describing The Little Light Project, in that she was a sensitive, intuitive child. I always knew my intuitiveness. I was very strong in feeling at a very early age. I can remember all that.

But when she started to define what that is, and I went *wow!* In fact, a very loose title for my upcoming book, which is still in its early stages, is called *Misunderstood*. I felt that I was misunderstood as a child, and this is what's happening. She's created it for parents to help them raise sensitive intuitive children and also understanding why they are the way they are.

When you understand these aspects of yourself, then you become more clear and understand why you are as you are. With that said, I accepted the invitation to be the vice president on the board to help share their message because it takes a village. There is also the grieving parent aspect of the non-profit. She's got a very dynamic group of people from professional therapists to holistic healers, all to be there. That's what we're striving to build it up and to address childhood sexual abuse, which unfortunately is rather rampant in society.

There again, that empathy inside of me and my heart aches for the victims of childhood sexual abuse.

Caren: When you started to tell me about all of this, you actually made an introduction for me because I was just so intrigued by what you were saying. In fact, I too have come from a world of not understanding what it was that I was feeling.

I am an empath I have discovered that now as I've gotten older. I am intuitive. I always knew I was intuitive. And then I started seeing the same things with my son who is now 29 and he was doing certain things as well.

I would text him, and he would immediately think and actually be right that something was wrong, even though I had never actually said anything was wrong, other than *Hi Rob, how are you? Let's get on the phone. I haven't talked to you in a while.*

Immediately he would go there. In fact, there was a reason he went there. There was something else. In fact, I didn't mention it. So there's that being intuitive and being an empath and how it can make your life a little crazy, quite frankly.

Nancy: It can. I draw upon the quote that knowledge is power. Once you have an understanding of what it means, what others are going through, I am in alignment with the fact that we teach what we need to learn. I found out throughout my coaching business, that I'm constantly learning from others, and I see a reflection of what they're experiencing.

I never question why people come into my life, for whatever reason, even if it's just a casual conversation. There is always something to be learned and then anchor what I've learned to help others.

That was a big part of why I became involved with The Little Light Project so I am able to help people that come to The Little Light Project for support. The webinars, workshops, and live events are created for those who need answers and support.

130

Caren: How do people find out more about the project? Is there a website we can send them to? I know we're in the middle of our interview, but while we're doing this, let's send them a link.

Nancy: Yes. It's http://LittleLightProject.org. It is an official non-profit organization and there is a donation section if your readers are feeling a call to donate. It all adds up to help us help others.

Caren: I think that's great, go check it out and see what this is all about. I know I'm going to be getting involved after having a wonderful conversation with one of the individuals who is involved in this. And again, thanks for this introduction that you have made for me.

So let's back up for just a little bit. What do you tell people that come to you either via coaching or maybe you see them on social media or they listen to you on your radio show, and they say, *I've lost my passion, I've lost my way, I don't know what I'm going to do next? What's my next step? I'm feeling desperate. I'm feeling depressed.* Any number of those things. I get those calls all the time.

What do you tell people when they do that?

Nancy: If they came to me with those questions, I would begin with, *just breathe and be still.* Let's get into your space of center to quiet down the noise within the mind and within the environment. Decibels of noise are even more amplified due to digital and electronic devices such as are here in my office. However, they are not in my bedroom, which is where I allow my mind to settle into quiet and my heart and soul to be in peace without interference.

It's a lot of energy, a lot of input. So when I connect with someone who says, what I shared earlier about me, really who am I? What is my purpose in life? Truly ask those questions.

When we start working together, most often I will begin with a vision board, because it is a very meaningful and enlightening experience for them. All I ask is that they come in with an open heart and an open mind. Bring these pictures that you don't know why you chose them. Because that's the key of it. This is your right brain right here. This is where you overthink.

I've had clients say, I don't know why I picked a particular image and I remind them that I gave them permission not to think. Shut the noise. And so we bring forth into an 8.5x11 piece of paper. *Wow! That's way too small.* You just said you were way too overwhelmed. We're here to laser focus, to find, to rediscover that GPS system within, which is also our intuition, our inner guide that we have stopped listening to, that we're living in the *I should be,* or *if I had done this.*

All that language of, *Wow I just get so exhausted.* Let's just rip that up energetically and put it in this box right now, because it's not serving you. Simplify and clarify your life so that you get a better visual of who you are, where you're going in life, and be open to receive.

That is huge, because it's already there.

Caren: It is. So people want to work on a vision board, probably say they could connect with you and you could walk them through that. I know that there are books out there. But you really believe in the vision board process. I do too. I don't use vision boards, I use vision cards. I do a slightly different thing, because I'm constantly updating it.

But again, can you give us a definition of what a vision board really is, so people that are listening and they hear this and they say, oh, *that sounds kind of interesting.* But what is a vision board exactly?

Nancy: There again, it's a snapshot of truly what it is that's already been inside of you. You just haven't been aware of it, like I shared with you. I forgot that I was wanting to be in media. Six years ago I would

132

have said, *crazy. That's just not possible.* I didn't have the awareness of it.

As I started applying my visions without knowing why, things would start naturally appearing. We want to know that there is a path. We always talk about that. We're on a journey. We're on a path. And we get off that path or we splinter and we don't know which way to go.

This starts activating your senses, your awareness, your visual, and your hearing. All of a sudden what you may have started blocking out, you release those headsets.

Caren: Would you agree, it's like a living, breathing entity?

Nancy: Yes. You have to keep vision boards. Like right now, I'm looking at mine right behind this computer screen. It's activated. This one was created purely by inspiration, because I'm working on more of my spiritual self within my writing. I'm doing a divine dialogue writing, which is very powerful.

I do energy work as well. When you have your chakra system, which are really your energy meridians, if they're out of balance, so is everything else. We need to bring our life back into balance. What I can say for sure is that it's very rare that I can say it's 100% success rate in that I can actually see an uplift if they're coming in feeling -

And it depends. Sometimes it's either through their body I can tell or they verbally will tell me that *I'm just not really sure what's going on in my life.* And I say, *let's just open up to the possibilities.* All of a sudden, they just start - their shoulders get back up, and they -

Sometimes it's very crystal clear what they have forgotten. Then they get into action. So being activated to it is by having it right in front of you. Now that we have smart phones and iPhones, you take a picture. I say, take a picture of your vision board. Look at it. When you're traveling, you don't have to bring that piece of paper around.

133

I used to take a snapshot, bring it to Kinko's and carry it as a picture in my purse, just to remind me. Because sometimes we can default, especially when you're starting to move forward. You're going to expect that. I wrote a blog on green light, red light. It's when you're going, then *boom!* Something will happen, and you may go back to that old pattern of thinking. This is going to shift you in that positive. Remember how you felt when you created this. This is you.

Caren: I hear you. And as I said, I use cards. So I'll go out and get a card, and I will create in that card *I am* statements. *I am so forth and so on.* Because our subconscious recognizes the present rather than the future or the present. It represents the present.

So if you talk in the present, *I am a highly successful sought-after motivational speaker,* your brain says, *oh that must be what you are.* And if your brain says, *I am making x amount of dollars,* or *I am living in this particular house,* and you visualize it -

I actually create these cards, and then I mail them to myself. I do them quarterly. I have a selection of all of my intentions, basically. I'm able to track it, because it changes.

Nancy: It changes every second of the day. 86,400 seconds that we're constantly changing. I am also very much an advocate of affirmations, but you have to believe it. Otherwise it's insignificant and inauthentic if you don't believe in your affirmations.

Be very intentional in that. When you are, then you already own it. Someone did this for me. They said, *Nancy, tell them what you do.* I said, *I host my radio show on internet talk blog radio.* And she said, *nope, we're cutting it down, because we want to define you better. Nancy, you are a radio personality.*

At that moment, it was like, *am I?*

Caren: Believe it.

134

Nancy: What does that increase? Our confidence. When we're talking about being vulnerable because of where we're at, and to think at that we move and change, it's been that steady progression. We have that choice to go back down by continuing because there's so much to experience. That's what activates me every day, is what's the next step?

Sometimes we're on a landing for a little while. Things happen in life. That's what I had to learn. We're all human. We go through the same experience.

Caren: Exactly. I totally agree with you. One of the things that I am very fond of and anyone who sees any of my social media knows that I like quotes. I like quotes that are not always inspirational. Sometimes they're funny and laughter is so needed in our lives.

I like quotes because they provide focus for the day, something to think about, something to think outside myself, something bigger than me, maybe it's something a famous person wrote. Maybe it's something a less than famous person wrote, a friend.

But today's quote that I want to share with you, and then I'm going to ask you to share with us maybe a quote that touches your heart. Today's quote was by John Maxwell, and he writes, *a great leader's courage to fulfill his vision comes from passion not position.*

What do you think about that?

Nancy: I have his book. It was right there. It might be here. My books travel through the night, kind of like the Nutcracker, and they show up where they need to. But yes, I was highlighting his book about something about how to be successful. He's very much into creative thinking and the big picture of life and being very passionate with that vision.

Our most modern visionaries, Steve Jobs and Walt Disney, are prime examples of stepping into your vision and believing in it so strongly that it's going to actualize itself without a doubt.

You can't take someone's passion away which is why I talk a lot about values. If you have 10 values down, and I tell you to take out five. *What? I can't do that.* And you've got one left. Everything defaults under it. For example, if someone tried to take away my integrity, I would jump off this house and go get it back.

No, you're not taking that away from me. So then you become even clearer about what you're all about.

Caren: Yeah, I understand that. It makes a lot of sense.

I have one more question for you, and this is kind of a fun question. If you could spread passion dust anywhere around the world on anyone around the world, who would you spread it on and what would you hope to accomplish?

Nancy: I actually do that every day, because I interview and I right now can't remember who shared that with me. There's such a need for love and passion - those two words are precious to me.

I know that my love and light will land exactly where it needs to be. But where I'm passionate about, I could say the world, but for right now in this conversation is for women to truly embrace who you are, that you don't need to measure up to anyone else.

Really be in that space of self-love, because that's the greatest gift you can give yourselves. As I shared with you earlier, it pains me to see someone that's been so broken down but yet I can see that light and I know that once they can get to that light, magic happens. So that's what I send with love and light.

Caren: I love that! I know that you have a free something, a complimentary gift that you want to give to any of our readers that are interested in receiving. It's absolutely complimentary. And it's called *Discover the Essence of You*. It's an audio mp3 and you just would like people to have this.

The way they can get that is to email you at Nancy@NancyFerrari. com. First of all you'll get an email from Nancy, and I know she'll respond to you. Second, you'll get a copy of *Discover the Essence of You*. It's an mp3 audio.

I love these kind of things because I put them on my smart phone. I always have something to listen to. I don't think I have this one, so I'm going to be emailing you as well Nancy, because I want to get a copy of this as well.

Any last thoughts that you'd like to share with our audience or let them know how they can reach you or just some last thoughts?

Nancy: It truly has been a divine pleasure to be spend time with you and just knowing that our messages collectively that we share are being heard is so important. With that said, I encourage everyone to also find their voice.

I had the distinct pleasure of interviewing Maryanne Williamson for a mere but meaningful 10 minutes. She told me there have been women throughout the centuries who have sacrificed their lives for their voice to be heard. Pioneers that have been before us who are still with us, and yet we remain silent.

It's time to remove the invisible shackles. You have so much to share. You have the brilliance within you and cast away the fears of judgment, being ostracized. Be in your power, because I know everyone has something. You matter. That's what I get. There was something that triggered me - I think this is going to surprise you.

There was a trigger during an interview. She's the founder of what's called *Your Soul Story* and she does some pretty in-depth work. It came up that I believed that I was nobody until I became somebody. As you can hear, this disempowering old belief brings down my voice because I lost my power just even thinking about it. The good news is that I've done the work to release the limiting belief. I am somebody and am proud of proclaim it!

In essence, they're just words. It's an old story. We were all put on this earth because we are somebody. We're somebody special. So never forget that.

Caren: Nancy, thank you. Truer words have never been said by somebody so powerful as you. I really appreciate what you have to share with us and who you are as an individual. I know that our listeners are going to gain so much by getting to know you.

I want to thank you from the bottom of my heart for sharing. I know you are very, very busy. I appreciate your willingness to come onto *The Passion Point* today and to share your vision and your thoughts and your life hopes with all of our listeners.

And a message to our readers. We know that you have many, many choices as to how you spend your time. Both of us are so appreciative that you decided to spend your time with us today. Ao as we say every single week, we look forward to hearing and seeing you back on the next show, *The Passion Point*, very, very soon. Have a great day everyone. Bye bye.

ABOUT THE AUTHOR

For the past 30 years Caren Glasser has dedicated her personal and professional life to communicating and connecting with people. Her past experiences have allowed her to meet many different people and make a difference in their lives. In the early 90's she was a children's rock and roll singer, signed with Rhino Records. She traveled the country singing songs of self-esteem. That experience culminated with a concert at Carnegie hall. During that same time she owned a creative arts company that provided programming for the public and private schools sector in Los Angeles. She has learned a lot about what it takes to create positive experiences in our lives. Today, as the founder of Promote Your Passion™, she focuses on helping people find their passion and create better lives for themselves.

Contact Caren and PYP Publishing at:

Caren@PromoteYourPassionNow.com

www.ingramcontent.com/pod-product-compliance
Lightning Source LLC
LaVergne TN
LVHW021345080426
835508LV00020B/2128